The New
Basset Hound

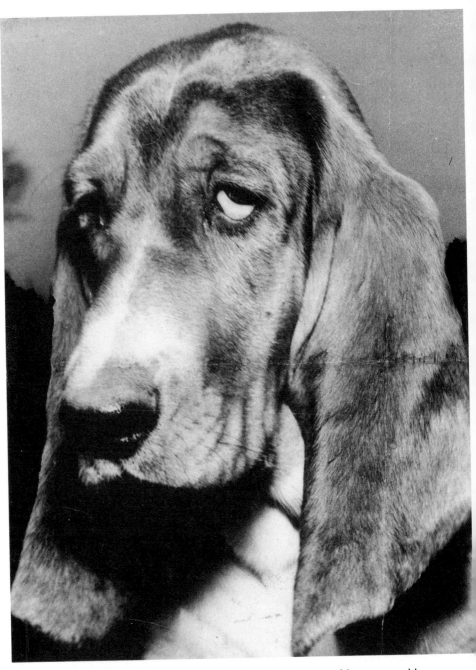

Ch. His Lordship of Lyn Mar Acres, by Lyn Mar's Actor ex his own granddam Ch. Duchess of Greenly Hall. Photo taken at 6 months of age.

The New
Basset Hound

Margaret S. Walton

HOWELL BOOK HOUSE

New York

Maxwell Macmillan Canada
Toronto

Maxwell Macmillan International
New York   Oxford   Singapore   Sydney

Howell Book House
Macmillan Publishing Company
866 Third Avenue
New York, NY 10022

Maxwell Macmillan Canada, Inc.
1200 Eglinton Avenue East
Suite 200
Don Mills, Ontario M3C 3N1

Macmillan Publishing Company is part of the Maxwell Communication Group of Companies.

Library of Congress Cataloging-in-Publication Data

Walton, Margaret S.
  The new basset hound / by Margaret S. Walton.
    p.   cm.
  Includes bibliographical references.
  ISBN 0-87605-022-4
  1. Basset hound. I. Title.
SF429.B2W35   1993
636.7'53—dc20
                                                                93-15114
                                                                CIP

Macmillan books are available at special discounts for bulk purchases for sales promotions, premiums, fund-raising, or educational use. For details, contact:

Special Sales Director
Macmillan Publishing Company
866 Third Avenue
New York, NY 10022

10 9 8 7 6 5 4 3 2 1

Printed in the United States of America

Contents

This book is dedicated
to the memory of
MILTON LYNWOOD WALTON
who wanted a Basset
and founded a dynasty

About the Author

MY MOTHER, Margaret Miller Stuart, was born into a family of animal lovers. Her father bred Standardbred horses and, being a Scotsman, always had Collies but never showed them. His brother was a veterinarian who specialized in large animals.

Her mother loved dogs, but her love of horses was confined to having a fine driving horse, although her father had bred carriage horses, mainly Hackney Cobs and German Coach.

Mother grew up with Collies and a Wirehaired Fox Terrier and always had a mare of her own and cats. She whelped her first litter at age thirteen when her older sister went on a business trip, leaving her with a very pregnant Chow Chow, promising to be back in time for the whelping—famous last words!

At age fourteen, mother was given an ''unentered'' English Foxhound, an independent, stubborn dog hound who refused to get along with the rest of the pack. He did, however, adore his new owner to the point of obsession. When he got a front paw caught in a trap, he merely ripped the trap from its peg and came home on three legs and waited for his mistress to get home from school and remove it, refusing to allow anyone else to touch him. This was my mother's introduction to hound temperament and devotion.

Following graduation and a couple of years in the business world, mother met and married a "Beagler"—Milton Lynwood Walton—who had a strong desire to own and hunt over a Basset Hound, having done so as a youngster.

Having been raised in horses, where soundness was always important, mother first studied all she could find on the breed. She contacted all known American kennels, received some interesting letters in return and took over a year to seek out just the right bitch.

When she was offered Duchess of Greenly Hall and my parents saw her at Westminster in 1943, they wanted to take her home immediately. But she was being shown by noted Beagle breeder Lee Wade, who had no authority to let her go, so it took a phone call the next morning before my parents were assured that Duchess was theirs—with certain provisions.

Having been taught by horsemen that children "keep their mouths shut and their ears open, thus learning much," my mother absorbed all that the great early breeders offered.

My father's love was the field, where he could hear his hounds run. Occasionally he would shoot a rabbit or hare, but it was mainly the sport of the chase that interested him.

My father, who enjoyed the puppies, went to only a few shows. He preferred to entertain Basset friends following a show, field trial or hunt. It was he who encouraged my mother to apply for her judging license in 1962 after observing what he considered "a horrendous example of how *not* to judge a Basset Hound."

Mother has judged in sixteen countries on five continents and the largest Specialty in one day—the Basset Hound Club of England, with 364 entries. She founded a regional Basset club and an all-breed club as well. She has bred five all-breed Best in Show winners and owned a sixth. My sister and I owned two of these.

Mother credits her knowledge of the breed to those who went before her and kindly took her under their wing. Some of these individuals are acknowledged in the last chapter. In her effort to learn as much as she can, mother has amassed a tremendous library on the breed.

It is hoped that some of the half-truths that have been written over the years will be laid to rest with this book and that the breed will make a strong comeback in the years to come.

—JOHN STUART WALTON

The author's introduction to the Basset Hound, Spring 1942.

Introduction

THIS BOOK is written after fifty years of breeding and showing Basset Hounds. It is offered as a guide for those people thinking of owning, showing, breeding or running a hound in the field. As a companion or an Obedience dog a Basset can only be considered a character! They love to try your patience and outwit you, turn a deaf ear to your pleas and refuse to believe they are not larger than anything around. They are loyal, devoted and wonderful baby-sitters for any age. In the field they have great stick-to-itiveness, slow and steady either on game or, as they were used in World War II, in locating land mines.

Once you have been owned by a Basset it is forever.

—PEG WALTON

Acknowledgments

I{T HAS BEEN SAID "No man is an island," and so it is when one is doing a book. All who contribute, even a small amount, make up the whole.

Much of this text is based not only on experience but also on research done over the years by others now gone but never forgotten, who passed on to us their knowledge, photos, prints and memorabilia. Al Michel presented us with very early photos; the late Kay Ellenberger (Tallyrand Kennels) willed me her entire dog and horse collection; Marianne Rosson, sister of the late Frank Hardy, entrusted me with the Hardys' photographic collection and other items, for which I humbly thank her.

Thank you to John Evans, ex Master of Basset Hounds for the Basset Hound Club (England) pack, who thrust into my hands and keeping a fantastic collection of photos and articles dating from the mid-nineteenth century.

Our veterinarian, Dr. Calvin Moon, always willing to pass on helpful information or advice, who has probably seen more Bassets and their problems than most of us see in a lifetime and was willing to put it to paper and have it published here.

Dick and Pat Waterhouse, who amassed enough information

and photographs to do their own book on Bassets in Canada, which had to be condensed.

Howard and Blackie Nygood, breeders, exhibitors, handlers and Basset lovers, who wrote two wonderful chapters complete with how-to photos. Their knowledge and ability to breed and show dogs of great type is legendary.

Elaine and Jerry Rigden, Betty Redmond, Rick White, Marg Patterson, Mike and Suzanne Sosne, Ginny and Frank Kovalic, all of whom were generous with information and photos.

The late, great photographer Rudolph W. Tauskey, who gave me wonderful photos of hounds behind our hounds. I will always remember and cherish his visits.

Kay and Craig Green, who gave freely of their time in compiling the chapter on Obedience and Tracking, and all those who generously supplied photos.

Last, but not least, to my son, who gave of his time and journalistic skills to help with this book.

Thank you all.

—PEG WALTON

The New
Basset Hound

Old print of George Krehl's Basset Hound "Pallas II" from "The Illustrated Sporting and Dramatic News, May 31, 1884"

1
History of the Breed

TO TRULY UNDERSTAND any breed, one should always go back to the origin and come forward, exploring every step of the way. With Bassets we must go back to France and realize that all small, low-set, dwarfed dogs were called Bas-set whether they were hounds, turnspits or terriers. "Bas-set" is translated as low set.

Every early author on the breed and even those who have written more recently concede that the breed stems from the old Talbot Hound, which was apparently also referred to as the St. Hubert. These had long, pendulous ears, deep lips, broad mouths and smooth coats. The one fact early writers cannot agree on is the color of these hounds. Richardson on *The Dog* (1860) states, "His color was usually pure white," but James Watson quotes these lines from Sir Walter Scott: "Two dogs of black St. Hubert's breed— unmatched for courage, breath and speed." Sir Jardine in *Hounds of the World* quotes King Charles IX (1550–1574) with writing, "The black hounds are of medium stature. The real breed of them have red or fawn marks over their eyes." All of this points to the fact that even at the turn of the century, Bassets were required to be tri-color or hare-pied.

Four small bronzes showing breed differences.

COMMON ANCESTORS

That the Basset and Dachshund were originally from common ancestry no early writer will deny. In E. Fitch Daglish's book on the Basset he writes, "De Fouilloux explains the title Basset d'Artois by which they were known, by telling us that the breed came originally from that province and near-lying Flanders. He divided them into two varieties—the Artesian, which had full-crooked forelegs, and the Flemish, which were straight-legged. The descendants of the Flemish type still exist in the Foret Noire, in the Voges and, I believe, in the German Dachshund which, according to my theory, is descended from Basset Hounds, which found their way into South Germany (Wurtemberg, the home of the Dachshund) via Alsace, and were there crossed with the terrier to give them that individual courage that is lacking in the hound. . . ."

In the same author's book on Dachshunds he describes two distinct types of this breed and writes: "The French naturalist Buffon (1793) described and figures both types, though the illustration of the crooked-legged dog is much more like a Basset Hound than a Dachshund; the animal being shown as lightly pied, big and houndy. On the other hand, the picture of the straight-legged type depicts a clearly recognisable Dachshund, but with a close, wire coat and unduly long legs."

Those who have seen the sketch by Louis Wain of The Dachshund and Basset Hound Show at the Royal Aquarium, Westminster, England, 1886, will notice the close similarity of the two breeds. With the exception of three distinct features, these two breeds are indeed closely allied. The distinct differences marking the Basset are, *size*—larger overall with more bone; *head*—being a "reduced" Bloodhound's—and *tail*—up rather than out.

Over the years we have enjoyed showing both Basset and Dachshund breeders a collection of small bronzes and have asked them to choose the breed. With the exception of the small brace, which is obviously Dachshund, the result in selection was about fifty-fifty. You now may judge them for yourself.

IMPORTATION INTO ENGLAND

The breed progressed rapidly with its importation into England, and we have Sir Everett Millais to thank for his dedication to this new breed. It has been written that he spared neither time nor money in an effort to do it justice. Unfortunately, as happens with a restricted gene pool, Millais realized he had to resort to an outcross, and so on advice from a prominent judge, Mr. Lort, he crossed Model with a Beagle, which seemed to prove successful. This is not a strange cross, as early prints show the Beagle of that time a totally different style of hound than we know today.

Lord Onslow also became interested in the Basset and imported two hounds from France, which gave fresh blood to the breeding programs of these two gentlemen. From these seems to have come the first lemon and whites in England; however, this color did not gain favor at that time—perhaps because the hound fraternity was more used to seeing the tri-color Foxhound, Beagle and Harrier.

The Basset became a popular pet and companion for many who seemed to delight in exhibiting at shows with entries ranging upward from fifty exhibits. The rough coat did not gain the same favor, although there were those who firmly believed in the "roughies" and championed their cause. It is interesting to note that from 1874 to 1900, 1,308 Bassets appear in the stud book while only 135 rough coats are listed. Some of both breeds were bred and owned by such well-known breeders as H.R.H. Prince of Wales, H. J. Stone, Capt. O. Swaffield, G. H. Krehl, Mrs. Tottie and Mons. Puissant. The Basset was definitely gaining ground as pet, show and pack hound, but small problems were brewing over the proper style of the breed.

IMPORTATION INTO THE UNITED STATES

Meanwhile, across the pond, America had a few Basset enthusiasts of its own. In the American Kennel Register, March 1884, we find:

> **Nemours**, tri-color dog, whelped March 21, 1883.
> Breeder—Mr. George R. Krehl, London.
> Owner—Mr. William Chamberlain, NY

In 1885 we find four more registered:

> **Bertrand**, tri-color dog, whelped April 14, 1884.
> Breeder—Mr. H. N. Watson, Cheshire, England.
> Owner—Mr. C. B. Gilbert, New Haven, CT

> **Diane**, tri-color bitch, whelped October 15, 1884.
> Breeder—Mr. Morris Burhams, Ulster County, NY
> Owner—Maizeland Kennels, Maizeland, Ulster County, NY

> **Jacques**, tri-color dog, whelped September 10, 1885.
> Breeder—Mr. Morris Burhams, Barreytown-on-Hudson, NY
> Owner—Maizeland Kennels, Dutchess County, NY

The latter two were sired by Nemours: Jacques out of Fleur de Lis, but Diane's dam was Burhams's Josephine, who had no registration number. Thus we are unsure if she was even a Basset!

> **Fleur de Lis**, tri-color bitch, whelped October 15, 1884.
> Breeder and owner—Mr. Morris Burhams, Dutchess
>   County, NY

This bitch is also by Nemours and the dam was again Josephine.

4

Basset Hound Club of America Field Trial, held at Kimberton, PA 1938. Kneeling is Fred Bayless with Ch. Chasseur; Mr. and Mrs. Lewis Thompson, Stanco pack, standing; next to Mrs. Thompson is Consuelo Ford, Bijou of Banbury pack.

Seven Bassets in 1886 were registered as follows:

> **Banderole**, tri-color bitch, whelped May 3, 1886.
> Breeder—Mr. Burnham [note the different spelling of this gentleman's name].
> Owner—Mr. John Stewardson, Philadelphia, PA
> Sire: Nemours
> Dam: Fleur de Lis
>
> **Louisette**, tri-color bitch, whelped May 3, 1886.
> Breeder—Mr. Burnham.
> Owner—Mr. R. H. Hart, Fern Rock, PA
> Sire: Nemours
> Dam: Fleur de Lis

Billy Bowlegs, black and tan dog, whelped April 19, 1885.
Breeder—Mr. B. F. Seitner, Dayton, Ohio.
Owner—Mr. A. Drunzer, NY
  Sire: Nemours
  Dam: Countess, by Nero out of Lotta

Canace, tri-color bitch, whelped August 14, 1884.
Breeder—Mr. F. P. Ellis, Thorleybourne, Bishop Stort-
    ford, England.
Owner—Mr. C. B. Gilbert, New Haven, CT
  Sire: Jupiter
  Dam: Citron, by Ch. Ramee out of Lord Onslow's
    Juno.

Fandango, tri-color dog, whelped September 2, 1886.
Breeder and owner—Mr. C. B. Gilbert.
  Sire: Bertrand
  Dam: Canace

Felicity, a litter sister to Fandango.
Breeder and owner—Mr. Gilbert.

Fannie, black, white and tan bitch, whelped September
    28, 1884.
Breeder—John F. Houser, Reynolds, PA
Owner—Harry S. Gilbert, Millersburgh, PA
  Sire: Imported Roger
  Dam: Imported Fannie

Whether the above two Mr. Gilberts were related I have no way of knowing.

For some unexplained reason there were no registrations for Bassets for the year 1887 but the breed had fanned interest in both the hunt field and the show ring. The report of the Philadelphia Dog Show, held September 16, 17, 18 and 19, has Dr. Downey as judge of both Beagles and Bassets. Interesting to note the report on the results:

Nemours of course took the Basset Hound prize and was taken out of the class to let the bench-legged beagles get a chance to win among themselves. This class we do not believe in, as it is evident they are a crossbred lot.

The report does not elaborate on just what they were crossed with!

The turn of the century found Bassets on a very slow course with owners coming and going as is usual in a newly introduced breed. Following World War I we find an upswing in the breed with Mr. and Mrs. Gerald Livingston importing a number of hounds from the famous Walhampton pack in England, as well as at least one couple of Basset d'Artois from France. In a conversation with Mr. Livingston he stated, ''The English hounds were excellent type and very beautiful but the French hounds were hell on rabbits.'' Thus he combined the two, making his pack tops in type and soundness as well as having great hunting ability—exactly what he had hoped to accomplish.

Mr. Erastus Tefft was also of the same mind but did not obtain the same results or stay in the breed for as long a time.

The Kilsyth Basset Hound pack Mr. and Mrs. Gerald Livingston, Joint Masters.

Dog's Name... Kilsyth Lucky ....Kennel Name ...Lucky............Sex...Male...........

Breed...Basset Hound........................Bred by...Owner......................................

Color...White & orange......................Whelped...January 9, 1942...Owner...Gerald M. Livingston...............

SIRE	SIRE	SIRE	SIRE
Kilsyth Baronet	Kilsyth Broker	Kilsyth Bunker	Ch.Walhampton Andrew
			DAM Belle
		DAM Kilsyth Fury	SIRE Governor
			DAM Kilsyth Dell
	DAM Kilsyth Brevity	SIRE Governor	SIRE Lanson
			DAM Ravaude
		DAM Kilsyth Actress	SIRE Ch.Walhampton Andrew
			DAM Walhampton Dainty
DAM	SIRE	SIRE	SIRE
Kilsyth Mitzi	Kilsyth Bob	Kilsyth Bunker	Ch.Walhampton Andrew
			DAM Belle
		DAM Kilsyth Fury	SIRE Governor
			DAM Kilsyth Dell
	DAM Kilsyth Frills	SIRE Prince of Kilsyth	SIRE Ch.Walhampton Andrew
			DAM Walhamton Dainty
		DAM Kilsyth Fanny	SIRE Kilsyth Bunker
			DAM Kilsyth Fury

8

Dog's Name **Basso of Banbury** Kennel Name **Basso** Sex **Male**

Breed **Basset Hound** Bred by **Consuelo U. Ford**

Color **Black, white & tan** Whelped **October 31, 1941** Owner **Lyn Mar Acres**

SIRE	SIRE	SIRE	SIRE
Ch. Bijou Rinestone of Banbury	**Ch. Chasseur**	SIRE Maple Drive Maxim	SIRE Walhampton Aaron
			DAM Baillet's Corvette
		DAM Maple Drive Topsy	SIRE Staridge Pol
			DAM Maple Drive Murky
	DAM Edwina	SIRE Ch. Reddy II	SIRE Reddy
			DAM Kilsyth Brevity
		DAM Walhampton Nicety	SIRE Walhampton Grazier
			DAM Walhampton Nicknack
DAM	SIRE	SIRE Kilsyth Bunker	SIRE Ch. Walhampton Andrew
Bijou Amethyst of Banbury	Kilsyth Banker		DAM Belle
		DAM Kilsyth Fury	SIRE Governor
			DAM Kilsyth Dell
	DAM Stanco Liz	SIRE Ch. Reddy II	SIRE Reddy
			DAM Kilsyth Brevity
		DAM Walhampton Nicety	SIRE Walhampton Grazier
			DAM Walhampton Nicknack

The Bijou of Banbury pack, Consuelo Ford, MBH, with four couple of Bassets. Tail hound is Bijou Rhinestone of Banbury; 5th from Master is Bijou Moonstone of Banbury. Note the "Jones Terrier" in the foreground.

The east coast seemed to be the stronghold of the Basset for many years with the Porters' **UPLAND** pack, Livingstons' **KIL-SYTH**, Slones' **BROOKMEAD**, Thompson's **STANCO** and Mrs. Ford's **BIJOU OF BANBURY**. Slowly the breed moved farther west with Carl Smith and Loren Free joining the ranks of Basset owners and breeders, although both of these gentlemen were primarily interested in hunting hounds and not necessarily show or pack.

By the 1930s the breed had really taken hold of a certain section of the hunting fraternity, never to let loose. From then on many have contributed to the breed and it would be impossible to name them all here. We will simply say "Thank you."

EARLY BREED HISTORY IN FRANCE
AND BELGIUM

In order that we further understand the breed in early France and Belgium it has been stated that "any hound standing lower than 16 inches—no matter from which province—is called a Basset."

The Bassets in these two countries were divided into three classes:

Bassets à jambes droites (straight-legged)
Bassets à jambes demi-torses (with forelegs half crooked)
Bassets à jambes torses (forelegs fully crooked)

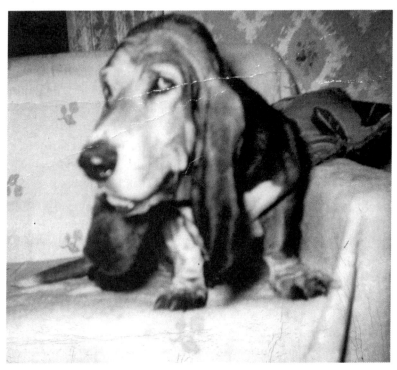

Ben's Black King—the sire of Ch. Webb's Black Amanda, who was the dam of Ch. Siefenjagenheim Lazy Bones.

In each of these three divisions were to be found three varieties of coats:

Bassets à poil ras (smooth-coated)
Bassets à poil due (rough-coated)
Bassets "half griffon" (a class of half rough-, half smooth-coated)

Types of the above varied from province to province but the general characteristics were nearly the same. All well-bred Bassets have true "hound heads" and long, pendulous ears, but the crooked-legged ones always seemed to show the better points than the straight-legged ones. It is interesting to note at this point that in all research the word "crooked" has been used, and it was not until the English took over the breeding that the fronts improved and the word "crooked" was eliminated.

One early French breeder tells us that if people wished to breed a good Basset, à jambes torses, they were obliged to be very careful in selecting the stock to breed from, if they did not wish the experiment to end in failure, for, should there be the slightest admixture of foreign blood, the "bar sinister" would be shown at once in the forelegs.

This then proves that the early Basset breeders encouraged crooked fronts and their description of hunting proves that fact. The Basset was always described as the slowest of hounds, this style of hunting being called "peculiar" in that the Basset wanted to hunt in its own way, and each hound wanted to do it individually and not blindly follow each other when one gave tongue. An owner of a number of hounds gave an account of his day in the field, stating that it was not uncommon to see the little hounds, when following a "mazy" track, crossing each other's route without paying any attention to one another; each of them working as though they were alone. This gentleman attributed this to their slowness and to their extremely delicate powers of scent, and to their innate stubborn confidence in their own powers. This tendency has certainly carried through all these years, as the stubborn confidence is still seen today in our own Bassets.

While any hound under 16 inches may have been called a Basset, the average "crooked-legged" Basset was normally between 10 and 15 inches at the shoulder, long-bodied, with very crooked front legs that had little more than an inch or two of daylight between the knees, stout thighs, gay sterns, "conical" heads, long faces and ears long enough to overlap each other by an inch or two (and sometimes more) when they were drawn over the nose. The front was described as "forepaws wide and well turned out," which certainly tells us how slow the Basset must have been with such a front!

In their native countries they were used on such game as deer, roebuck, wild boars, wolves, foxes, hares and rabbits, but if trained exclusively on one species of game they would not run anything else. One gentleman wrote he had been hunting with a Basset on hare, and the hound "ran through fifty rabbits and never noticed them."

The French Provinces

In Brittany, Vendée, Alsace, Lorraine and Luxemburg, where cover was dense and very rough, the semi-crooked Bassets were used. The owners and breeders found these to have every bit the nose of the smaller Basset and claimed they ran a bit faster but not so that they lost the game. Further, they were able to jump the ditches rather than go down into them and then have to scramble up the other side as did the lower, fully crooked–fronted hound.

The above hounds were different in type than the lower ones in that the lips were shorter as were the ears, the skull was less conical and the occiput not nearly as pronounced; the body was shorter and the stern was carried in a horizontal position, the feet were rounder and they carried less bone. They were also more on the leg, some going to 16 inches. One Frenchman wrote that he believed the cross to be that of the "regular hound" and the Basset à jambes torses. Obviously this was a cross that worked for the hunter in a certain type of terrain, just as the "English Basset" was developed for nearly the same reason by crossing the Basset with Beagle and Harrier many, many years later and in another country.

One gentleman who at one time wrote under the nom de guerre of ''Snapshot,'' and who was better known to many of the ''doggy'' men as ''Wildfowl,'' had considerable knowledge of the Continental hound. He has written that ''a black and tan or a red Basset à jambes torses cannot, by any possible use of one's eyes, be distinguished from a Dachshund of the same colour. Although some German writers assert that the breeds are quite distinct. To the naked eye there is no difference.

''But in the matter of names (wherein German scientists particularly shine), then indeed, confusion gets worse confounded. They have, say, a dozen black and tan Bassets à jambes torses before them. Well, if one of them is a thorough good-looking hound, they call this one Dachs Bracken; if one is short-eared and with a pointed muzzle, they cap that one with the appellation of a Dachshund.

''Between you and me, kind reader, it is a distinction without a difference, and there is no doubt that both belong to the same breed. I will, at a fortnight's notice, place a Basset à jambes torses, small size, side by side with the best Dachshund Hound to be found, and if any difference in legs, anatomy and general appearance of the two can be detected, I shall be very greatly surprised. That the longer-eared and squarer-muzzled hound is the better of the two for practical work there is not the shadow of a doubt; but, of course, if digging badgers is the sport in view, then the Dachshund Terrier is the proper article. But that is not to be admitted. One *cannot* breed Hounds from Terriers, whereas one *can* breed Terriers from Hounds, and therefore the Dachshund Terrier is descended from the Basset à jambes torses. As for Dachshund Hounds, they are, in every respect, Basset à jambes torses; at least, that is the opinion I have come to after a great deal of experience.

''Quarrelling about names is an unprofitable occupation. Never mind the 'Bracken' or the 'Hund,' since the two articles are alike. I say, from the evidence of my senses, that they must come from the same stock, and since they cannot come from a Terrier pedigree, the Hound one is the only logical solution.''

The Basset à jambes droites has been described looking more like a Beagle and some even refused to consider them being called Bassets. They had a much shorter face, broader flat ears, slightly longer neck, short back, very level from shoulder to rump and tails carried straight up. This description is more like the Beagle or Harrier than that of a Basset, and it was understandable that many sportsmen refused to consider this a "Basset." They have been described as not being as interesting to hunt over as they were fast and often overran the check, but it was stated that for fast fun, exercise and music, they would do.

ORIGINAL FUNCTION

I have always been fascinated by the use of the Basset in the early days. I simply cannot imagine our hounds of today hunting wolves or wild boar, and yet there are documented reports of just this type of hunt. One early writer stated he had the pleasure of killing two wolves that were, individually, hunted by one Basset. He went on to say that it showed extraordinary pluck on the part of the little hound; for be it known that, as a rule, any hound or dog who comes for the first time on the scent of a wolf forthwith bolts home, or hides behind the master for protection.

Bassets have also been used for shooting birds, and it is interesting to note that when this was done, the hound's collar was fitted with a bell, or a small brass "grelot," so that the shooter would know the location of the hound. We had one Basset who, when following the scent of a pheasant, totally changed his tone of voice. We always knew what he was on and he never failed us.

One use of the Basset which is most interesting to me was that of the "truffle hound." Training for this has been described as wonderfully simple and was apparently developed by the peasants of France. When young, the hound is kept a day without food, and a truffle shown to the dog on that day. The peasant then throws it into some small covert, hides it in stones or perhaps buries it lightly in the ground and makes the dog find it. When the dog has done so, the peasant gives him a piece of bread.

This is repeated until the Basset readily looks for the truffle. The dog is then taken to those places in the neighborhood where truffles are known or suspected to be, and the peasant, pretending

Am. and Bermuda Ch. Sir Tomo of Glenhaven, sired by Eleandon's Black Magic and out of Ch. Lyn Mar Acres Fyre Ball (a litter sister to Ch. L.M.A. Top Brass). Black Magic carried Greenly Hall and LMA lines. Bred by Eleanor Bliss and owned by John and Margretta Patterson and Emily Kultchar.

to throw away the usual truffle, tells the dog, "Cherchez-cherchez!" ("Seek! Seek!"). At this point the little hound begins hunting around, comes upon a truffle scent and begins digging for the tuber (truffle). At the first sign of success on scent, the peasant goes in and digs out the precious fungus.

ORIGINAL FORM—NOT NECESSARILY
FOLLOWING FUNCTION

For a hundred or more years there has been the debate on just why the Basset has had "crooked legs." Buffon and other old French authorities held that the crooked legs were the result of rickets. In the *Dictionnaire d'Histoire Naturelle* it was stated that the crooked-legged variety was esteemed the best and that this originated in a malady similar to "rachitis," which was transmitted as a deformity to their descendants. It was finally held to be indicative of purity as we find in *La Chasse au Tir*, Paris, 1827:

Deux Bassets bien dresses, Medor avec Brissant
Leur baroque structure
Vous announce déjà qu'ils sont de race pure.

As all abnormally long-bodied and short-legged dogs have a tendency to crooked forelegs in order to get balance, there is no

Ch. Promise Of Greenly Hall—Duchess of Greenly Hall at one year of age and Sir Guy of Greenly Hall who was offered as a pet.

reason to believe that Bassets got their crooked legs from rickets any more than neglected short-legged dogs, where selection of straight legs is made essential, became bad-fronted when selection was not attended to.

Unfortunately for the above theory, proper breeding and correct feeding programs have virtually eliminated the crooked-fronted Basset where they were so overdone that the chest was literally on the ground and the hound could barely walk. Further, many early hounds were indeed knuckled over because of the crooked front. With the Basset entering England and with the breeding knowledge of early terrier breeders, much help was obviously given in this department.

Another Theory

Another theory on fronts is much more extreme and gross, in my opinion. In the days of the cruel Forest Laws, implemented by the Saxons and continued by the Normans, all hounds owned by other than royalty were deliberately mutilated by duly authorized game wardens. This was supposedly to prevent poaching and hunting by commoners in the royal hunting parks and lands. This system of mutilation was barbaric, and entailed "the cutting-off of pads on the forefeet" and "the severing of sinews and tendons in the hind legs." Both of these certainly prevented hounds from running almost anything. The commoners decided to try breeding hounds so restricted by natural structure that they would not be subjected to the cruelty of the wardens. This resulted in the Basset Hound—extremely slow but still capable of hunting and killing small game.

You may or may not wish to believe the above explanation and I tell you it is indeed merely one theory set forth for you to ponder.

It is a known fact among Basset breeders that improper nourishment of either dam or the puppies results in damage to fronts. Puppies raised on cement, given overdoses of calcium, becoming ill at an early age, receiving an injury to the front legs, even in the whelping box, all contribute to a problem front.

I have seen puppies with good front and shoulder go off their feed for a brief period and the front seems to go. We are not speaking here of the hereditary factor of one turned front foot that those of us who have bred a few litters know of. We are looking at a totally malformed front, usually accompanied by being down in the pasterns and with the toes rolling up so that one sees the front of the pad.

It is a known fact that in the very early days of the Basset and other hounds, the feeding program was most interesting. One book speaks of "new milk, and biscuit, the rest he will forage for himself"; another speaks of raw meat and stale bread soaked in milk. One author even gives you an insight into the freedom allowed when quoted, "He ought to be a very good hound, because he ate the missus's petticoat and prayer book."

FUNCTION FITTING FORM

With the importation of the Basset into England and dedicated breeders such as Everett Millais and George R. Krehl, the breed changed course somewhat. By using first the Beagle and then the Bloodhound, Mr. Millais added a straighter front than he realized and, even though he states that within a few generations he had the Basset back on track, little did he realize that the straighter front would remain recessive.

In an article written by Fred. W. Blain, a well-known gentleman in the earlier days of the breed, his concern for the future of Bassets was made clear when he states: "Let me advise any one trying Bassets for hunting not to attempt to teach them with the whip and harsh words, as they are very sensitive, and easily frightened, and in some cases never forget a thrashing. Headstrong they certainly are, and fond of their own way—but this failing must be put up with; to those who know the breed they are not hard to manage, with a little tact.

"I consider that, in making use of Bassets to run as Beagles, we are taking them rather out of their element, and, consequently, it will take time before they can be expected to be perfect at this work. For shooting where the coverts are too dense for beaters,

Ch. Margem Hills For The Books was a very popular sire of both field and show hounds. He figured prominently in the pedigrees of Dr. and Mrs. Wisner's show dogs as well as in the Tantivy pack of the late Jane Luce. Bred by John and Margretta Patterson, he was a son of Ch. Sir Tomo Of Glenhaven ex Ch. Margem Hills Gollywog (Tomo ex Ch. Reveille's Moonbeam by Lazy Bones).

Bassets in France take the place of our Spaniels, driving everything before them, and making such a noice that neither boar nor rabbit is likely to remain in cover. This was, I think, their original use in France; but in this country game is generally too plentiful and highly preserved for them to be much used.

"I hope that, in breeding Bassets for hunting purposes, owners will not neglect the heavy and somewhat ungainly appearance that they should have, and gradually get them higher on the leg and lighter in bone and body; by so doing they may increase the speed, but they will lose the endurance, and they will in time be nothing better than deformed Beagles. I have already noticed a tendency in this direction in packs. If Bassets are not fast enough for a man, let him by all means keep Beagles instead. You cannot expect a Clydesdale to go as fast as a thoroughbred, nor would you think of breeding them to do so. Keep each to his real work: both are good, but their style may suit different tastes.''

Mr. Blain wrote the above at the turn of the century and I am sure he would be greatly shocked to see what has happened to his beloved breed were he able to return. He probably would be even more shocked to learn that Clydesdales have indeed been bred to the thoroughbred and the result has been some excellent ''hunter-hacks.'' I am sure he would decry the ''English Basset'' as an abomination even though it was bred for a specific style of hunting small game; nor would he approve of the fronts we now have (or should have) in which the ''crook'' is properly in the upper arm and the sternum rests within, just as it was described in the first English standard.

Ch. Tantivy Door Mouse, a member of the Tantivy pack, Jane Luce, MBH. Door Mouse was shown to her show championship by Dorothy Hardy.

Dual Ch. Kazoo's Moses The Great was the first to attain this honor. Bred by Mr. and Mrs. Shields and owned by Mr. and Mrs. James Dohr, Moses first won his Field title and was then handled by Jerry Rigden to his show championship.

Very little has been written about the rough variety of Bassets, but one of the earliest references I have ever come across was that a Mr. Higginson obtained two couples of this variety to see whether they would do as well as the Beagles used by the Middlesex Hunt of Massachusetts, but they did not give satisfaction and the hunt graduated to English Foxhounds. No further explanation was ever given, although it does seem rather obvious that stone walls, heavy cover and ditches do not make easy hunting grounds for the smaller hounds, no matter how tough a character they are.

EARLY U.S. BREEDING

As stated earlier, those who did bring the Basset to these shores for pack hunting had their work cut out for them in order to breed sound hounds of good type. I offer you the pedigrees in this chapter

The first dual Ch. bitch was Helwal's Desire, bred, owned and shown to both titles by Helen and Walter Smith. Desire first won her show title and, because she was used for hunting, the Smiths started to go to Field Trials. Desire was on her way to her Field title when she was struck by a car while hunting. For a period of two years she was unable to compete. Sired by Ch. Lyn Mar Acres Barrister ex Helwal's Hooligan.

from two top packs of the 1920s and 1930s to show how the imported hounds were used. Even today, packs work closely together in order that the best type with the best hunting ability be kept for the future of each individual pack. Any Master or Huntsman of a pack will tell you there are three words when breeding top hounds: BREED—FEED—WEED.

I have also included a pedigree of an import of the mid-1950s that will show you the effect of the French import into England and his son on to America. The late William Brainard saw this hound "Domino" at Crufts, where the hound placed Best of Breed, and decided he would be a great outcross for the Tewksbury Foot Bassets who, at that time, were still pure Bassets. We were honored to be allowed to breed a Lyn Mar Acres bitch to him prior to his entering the pack. This breeding produced four bitch puppies, all of whom were kept by us. At a later time, Betty Porter of the Upland pack

Dog's Name...Domino...........................Kennel Name ....Sex...Male.............

Breed...Basset Hound...........................Bred by...Col. Morrison.........................

Color Black blanket, white & tan Whelped May 14, 1951 Owner Tewksbury Foot Bassets

SIRE	SIRE	SIRE	SIRE
	Sans Souci de Bourceville	Nero de Bourceville	
			DAM
		DAM Ravaude de Bourceville	SIRE
			DAM
Grims Ulema de Barly	DAM Querelle de Barly	SIRE Mireau de Barly	SIRE
			DAM
		DAM Mirabelle de Barly	SIRE
			DAM
DAM	SIRE Westerby Rennet	SIRE Willoughby Roderick	SIRE
			DAM
		DAM Eastington Park Restless	SIRE
			DAM
Westerby Dorcas	DAM Westerby Damask	SIRE Westerby Rennet	SIRE
			DAM
		DAM Westerby Daybreak	SIRE
			DAM

24

imported Westerby Dominick to whom a Lyn Mar Acres bitch was also bred, and this resulted in Ch. Lyn Mar Acres Scalawag, a hound found in a number of the older pedigrees and breedings.

These pedigrees are only for reference on some of the early imports who contributed to the breed's future. There were others who were equally important, namely Ch. Rossingham Barrister, imported by Richard and Evelyn Basset of Washington State and Barrister's litter sister, Ch. Rossingham Blessing, brought over by Dorothy Benson of New York. Both of these hounds became American champions rather quickly and contributed greatly to the breed's future.

It is interesting to note that the charter members of the Basset Hound Club of America were comprised of those who enjoyed the hounds in the field. The Bissells, Livingstons and Thompsons all

Lyn Mar Acres deMarch, litter brother to Ch. Lyn Mar Acres Debutante, by Ch. Lyn Mar Acres Top Brass ex Ch. Debbie's Gift—both by Ch. Clown. Demi suffered a shoulder injury at 8 months of age and could not be shown but became a top sire. Bred and owned by Lyn Mar Acres.

owned very prominent and active packs; Mr. and Mrs. Seitz, Carl Nottke and Wilbur Klapp, Jr., were all interested in field work.

Perhaps this accounts for the sound Bassets of good type one saw in the 1930s and 1940s, as it was only when those primarily interested in "show dogs" that the breed started to be "overdone" in one area or another and the soundness and beautiful type began to disappear. How well I remember one hound in the 1940s who, according to the owner, "weighed 75 pounds," and I measured him at 17 inches with a head large enough for a Bloodhound. Not only was this animal used for breeding on numerous occasions, but I can even spot hounds today that revert back to him.

As the breed progressed westward, Dachshund breeders became interested in the breed, which seems perfectly natural. Grace Greenburg and Cordelia Skapinski Jenson became active breeders and did much to further the breed in California.

Mr. and Mrs. William Morris moved from the east coast to California with a job change and took with them Ch. Elnora of Lyn Mar. Bred to a west coast dog, she produced the TV star "Morgan," who had been sold and returned to the east. Later, the owner decided he would like to have Morgan shown and contacted Peter Knoop, a very well-known Doberman Pinscher breeder and professional handler. In their first show ring outing, Morgan met Lordship, our first linebred dog, who was doubled on Ch. Clown and sired by Clown's litter brother Actor. Lordship later became Ch. His Lordship of Lyn Mar Acres. We decided each hound should go in a different direction, thereby eliminating some chance of defeat for either one, both good hounds. On this note, Pete took Morgan north and Lordship and I stayed south. Both dogs finished easily, Morgan with only that one defeat, and became Ch. Sir Guy of Elwill.

The breed progressed rapidly in the 1950s partly because of the popularity of the new star "Cleo," of the TV show "The People's Choice." One of the most frustrating conversations to any breeder was the question, "Do your Basset puppies talk?" There were even those who wanted to try breeding "miniature Bassets," apparently wishing to compete with the miniature Dachshunds as an apartment-sized dog. Fortunately for the breed, this never got off the ground and little or nothing was heard of this again. We all know that popularity is the kiss of death for any breed and with all the publicity and exposure certainly Bassets jumped into the limelight in a great hurry. As usually happens when a breed takes hold, there were those who purchased bitches from anyone they could just to have litters and sell the puppies for as great a profit as possible.

Prior to this time we saw very few long-haired Bassets, but with this popularity they became so prevalent that at one time it was suggested that if these breeders wished to continue to produce longhairs, they should concentrate on doing so and perhaps try to make it a variety as was the long-haired Dachshund. Unfortunately for this suggestion, the long-haired Basset does not breed true and most were reluctant to try this experiment. With the disqualification in the new Standard taking effect for the show ring, and with the overpopulation of the Basset, longhairs are rarely seen today.

It seems most unfortunate that, while everyone is certainly entitled to their own style of Basset, the Standard is certainly not being adhered to in the show ring. Many of today's judges seem very confused when they find a ring full of hounds with perfectly flat chests with no apparent sternum bone—merely a lot of fat and loose skin, short necks and backs and extremely straight shoulders. All are faults and a steep shoulder is a serious fault, yet most judges are reluctant to penalize a hound for this.

For those of you who are now becoming part of Basset history and for years to come will help mold and shape the future of the breed, you must put into the show ring and the field only those hounds you honestly feel are closest to the Standard and can well do the job for which they are bred.

HEAD: Medium width, large, well-proportioned; length from occiput to muzzle greater than width at brow; skull well-domed; pronounced occipital protuberance; length of nose to stop approx. from stop to occiput; skull sides flat, free from cheek bumps. Side view: Top lines of muzzle and skull, straight, parallel; skin over entire head loose, distinct wrinkles over brow when head is lowered

EARS extremely long, low-set (far back on head); drawn forward, tips fold over end of nose; velvety; hang in loose folds; ends curling slightly inward

EYES slightly sunken, haw prominent; dark brown preferred (lighter, according to coat acceptable); light or protruding eyes, faults

STOP moderately defined

MUZZLE deep, heavy, free from snipiness; teeth large, sound, regular; scissors or even bite; overshot or undershot a serious fault; lips dark, pendulous, falling squarely in front; loose, hanging flews; dewlap very pronounced

SHOULDERS well-laid-back, powerful; set close against chest

CHEST deep, full; prominent sternum in front of legs; distance from chest to ground not to exceed one-third height at withers of adult

FORELEGS short, powerful; bone heavy; skin wrinkled; elbows set close against sides of chest

PAWS massive, very heavy; pads tough, heavy, well-rounded; feet inclined trifle outward; (down on pasterns, a serious fault); toes, neither pinched nor splayed; dewclaws may be removed

DISQUALIFICATIONS: Height of more than 15" at highest point of shoulder blades; knuckled-over front legs; distinctly long coat

COAT hard, smooth, short; density sufficient for all weather; skin loose, elastic

COLOR: Any recognized hound color

TAIL set in continuation of spine; not to be docked; carriage slight curvature, gay; hair on underside coarse

APPEARANCE: Short-legged, very heavy-boned; movement deliberate but not clumsy; of great endurance; temperament, mild, devoted

SIZE: Desired height not to exceed 14"

TOPLINE straight, level; free from sag or roach

NECK powerful, well-arched, of good length

NOSE dark, black preferred; nostrils large, wide open; liver-colored conforming to head color permissible but not desirable

RIBS well-sprung with adequate room for lungs, heart; rib structure long, smooth, extending well back

HINDQUARTERS very full, well-rounded; approx. equal to shoulder width; a firm stance, no crouching; hind legs straight; rear view, parallel; stifle, well-let-down; hocks turning neither in nor out; hind feet point straight ahead; dewclaws may be removed

Visualization of the Standard Reprinted from *Dog Standards Illustrated*, Howell Book House, 1975. Italian and American Champion Lyn Mar Acres M'Lord Batuff by Bats ex Lyn Mar Acres Sweet Stuff. He finished from the Puppy class and became a top producer and was bred, owned and shown by Margaret S. Walton. Later he was sold to Dr. Giuseppi Benelli of Italy. Three weeks after arriving, "Butch" won his first all breed Best of Show on the continent.

2

The Standard

ONE WEBSTER DEFINITION of Standard is: "The type, model or example commonly or generally accepted or adhered to; criterion set for usages or practices. A level of excellence, attainment, etc., regarded as a measure of adequacy."

To further explore this we find:

TYPE: A person, animal or thing that is representative of, or has the distinctive characteristics of, a class or group.

STYLE: Sort, kind, variety. The way anything is made or done.

STRAIN: A line of individuals of a certain species or race, differentiated from the main group by certain, generally superior qualities.

How often have you heard it said by exhibitors that they do not have that judge's TYPE of Basset when what they really mean is STYLE? In actuality, *type* is the Standard for the breed but *style* is your own interpretation of the Standard. A *strain*, therefore, is your bloodline, developed over years of trial and error, giving you what *you* believe the Basset should be.

The Standard for the Basset Hound has changed very little over the past one hundred years—the style of the Basset Hound most certainly has. The Standard at the turn of the century is as applicable today as it was in 1900.

GENERAL APPEARANCE

1. To begin with the head as the most distinguishing part of all breeds. The head of the Basset Hound is most perfect when it closest resembles a Bloodhound's. It is long and narrow, with heavy flews, occiput prominent, "la bosse de la chasse," and forehead wrinkled to the eyes, which should be kind, and show the haw. The general appearance of the head must present high breeding and reposeful dignity; the teeth are small, and the upper jaw sometimes protrudes. This is not a fault, and is called the "bec de lièvre."

2. The ears are very long, and when drawn forward folding well over the nose—so long, that in hunting they will often actually tread on them; they are set on low, and hang loose in folds like drapery, the ends inward curling, in texture thin and velvety.

3. The neck is powerful, with heavy dewlaps. Elbows must not turn out. The chest is deep, full and framed like a "man-of-war." Body long and low.

4. Forelegs short, about four inches, and close-fitting to the chest till the crooked knee, from where the wrinkled ankle ends in a massive paw, each toe standing out distinctly.

5. The stifles are bent, and the quarters full of muscle, which stands out, so that when one looks at the dog from behind it gives him a round barrel-like effect. This, with their peculiar waddling gait, goes a long way towards

Basset character—a quality easily recognised by the judge, and as desirable as Terrier character in a Terrier.

6. The stern is coarse underneath, and carried hound-fashion.

7. The coat is short, smooth and fine, and has a gloss on it like that of a racehorse. (To get this appearance, they should be hound-gloved, never brushed.) Skin loose and elastic.

8. The colour should be black, white and tan; the head, shoulders and quarters a rich tan, and black patches on the back. They are also sometimes hare-pied.

The above Standard is taken directly from:

The Basset Hound
Club Rules and Stud Book
compiled by
the Late SIR EVERETT MILLAIS,
corrected and made up to March 1900
by
Mrs. Mabel Tottie

As the breed became popular in the show ring in England, the dogs became more and more unsound in leg and movement. It was at this point that Captain Godfrey Heseltine took exception to the fact that head was most important and went so far as to say it was not so either in the Basset *or* the Dachshund, both of which are more distinguished from other hounds by the disproportion between their length and height than any other feature. He then compiled, in 1898, the following description for his puppy walkers:

HEAD—The head should be large, the skull narrow and of good length, the peak being very fully developed, a very characteristic point of the head, which should be free from any appearance of, or inclination to, cheek bumps. It is most perfect when it closest resembles the

Ch. The Ring's Ali Baba was one of the nation's top Group and Best in Show dogs. Bred by Robert and Mary Lees Noerr of The Ring's Bloodhound fame, Ali Baba was sold to Frances Scaife and was shown by Jerry Rigden. Sired by Ch. Long View Acres Smokey and out of Ch. Miss Linda Lovely of Elvalin.

head of a bloodhound, with heavy flews and forehead wrinkled to the eyes. The expression when sitting, or when still, should be very sad, full of reposeful dignity. The whole of the head should be covered with loose skin, so loose in fact, that when the hound brings its nose to the ground the skin over the head and cheeks should fall forward and wrinkle sensibly.

JAWS; NOSE—The nose itself should be strong and free from snipiness, while the teeth of the upper and lower jaws should meet. A pig-jawed hound, or one that is underhung, being distinctly objectionable.

EARS—The ears are very long, and when drawn forward, folding well over the nose. They are set on the head as low as possible and hang loose in folds like drapery, the ends inward curling, in texture thin and velvety.

EYES—The eyes should be deeply sunken, showing a prominent haw, and in colour they should be a deep brown.

NECK AND SHOULDERS—The neck should be powerful with heavy dewlaps set on sloping shoulders.

FORELEGS—The forelegs should be short, very powerful, very heavy in bone, close-fitting to the chest with a crooked knee and wrinkled ankle, ending in a massive paw. A hound must not be ''out at elbows,'' which is a bad fault.

FEET—He must stand perfectly sound and true on his feet, which should be thick and massive, and the weight of the forepart of the body should be borne equally by each toe of the forefeet so far as it is compatible with the crook of the legs. UNSOUNDNESS IN LEGS OR FEET SHOULD ABSOLUTELY DISQUALIFY A HOUND FROM TAKING A PRIZE.

CHEST AND BODY—The chest should be deep and full. The body should be long and low, and well-ribbed up. Slackness of loin, flatsidedness, a roach or razor back are all bad faults.

HOCKS—A hound should not be straight on his hocks, nor should he measure more over his quarters than he does at the shoulders. Cow hocks, straight hocks or weak hocks are all bad faults.

Ch. Halcyon Crackerjack, bred by L. & V. Steedle, owned by Ed Smizer and Gwen McCul-lagh and shown by Ed. "C.J." is the top Specialty winning Basset in the history of the breed.

Dog's Name ...**Ch. Halcyon Crackerjack**............ Kennel Name ..**C.J.**........ Sex ...**Male**...........

Breed ...**Basset Hound**............ Bred by ...**L. F. & V. L. Steedle**.........

Color ...**Black, white & tan**............ Whelped ...**January 22, 1978**.. Owner ...**Ed Smizer & Gwen McCullagh**.....

SIRE	SIRE	SIRE	SIRE
		Ch. Lyn Mar Acres End Man	
	Ch. Lyn Mar Acres Extra Man		DAM
		DAM Tantivy Demon	SIRE
			DAM
Ch. Halcyon Lumberjack	DAM	SIRE Ch. Blackie's Bleemer	SIRE
			DAM
	Ch. Tess von Skauton, CD	DAM Ch. Sacata von Skauton	SIRE
			DAM
DAM	SIRE	SIRE Ch. Stoneybluff Freckles	SIRE
			DAM
	Ch. Jagersven Benchmark	DAM Ch. Jagersven Blue Ribbon	SIRE
			DAM
Jagersven Marchesa	DAM	SIRE Ch. Jagersven Monarch II	SIRE
			DAM
	Jagersven Empress	DAM Ch. Jagersven Headliner	SIRE
			DAM

35

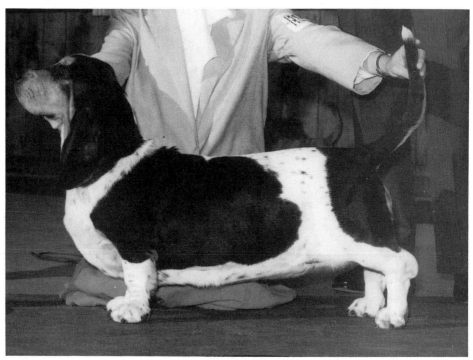

Ch. Stoneybluff Gertrude has been one of the top winning bitches in the breed. Winner of BOS at the BHCA National in 1987, BB in 1988 and 1989, she also won BB at the Pilgrim Specialty, 1987. She repeated this win three more times, shown by her handler Gwen McCullagh. Gertrude was bred and owned by Frank and Virginia Kovalic.

Dog's Name ... Ch. Stoneybluff Gertrude ... Kennel Name ... Gertrude ... Sex ... Bitch

Breed ... Basset Hound ... Bred by ... Owners

Color ... Black, white & tan ... Whelped ... May 3, 1982 ... Owner ... Virginia & Frank Kovalic

SIRE Stoneybluff Oliver	**SIRE** Stoneybluff Sherlock	**SIRE** Ch. Stoneybluff Ringer	**SIRE**
			DAM
		DAM Ch. Stoneybluff Desiree	**SIRE**
			DAM
	DAM Stoneybluff Gypsy	**SIRE** Stoneybluff Late Edition	**SIRE**
			DAM
		DAM Stoneybluff Caroline	**SIRE**
			DAM
DAM Stoneybluff Nikoma	**SIRE** Ch. Stoneybluff Ringer	**SIRE** Ch. Lyn Mar Acres End Man	**SIRE**
			DAM
		DAM Ch. Lyn Mar Acres Michelle	**SIRE**
			DAM
	DAM Stoneybluff Pocohontas	**SIRE** Jagersven Editor	**SIRE**
			DAM
		DAM Ch. Stoneybluff Antoinette	**SIRE**
			DAM

American Champion Walhampton Andrew, imported and owned by Gerald Livingston, Kilsyth pack.

QUARTERS—The quarters should be full of muscle, which stands out so that when one looks at the dog from behind, it gives him a round, barrel-like effect, with quarters "round as an apple." He should be known as "a good dog to follow," and when trotting away from you, his hocks bend well, and he should move true all round.

STERN—The stern is coarse underneath, and carried "gaily" in hound fashion, i.e., pothooked.

COAT—The coat should be similar to that of a foxhound, not too fine and not too coarse, but yet of sufficient strength to be of use in bad weather. The skin loose and elastic.

COLOUR—No good hound is a bad colour, so that any recognised foxhound colour should be acceptable to the judge's eye, and only in the very closest competition should the colour of a hound have any weight with a judge's decision.

When the Basset Hound Club of America was founded in 1933, most of the members' packs consisted of Walhampton hounds and thus the above Standard was used with very few changes. In The American Kennel Club's purebred dogs book of Standards (copyright 1935), we find Heseltine's Standard for the Basset Hound "by courtesy of the Basset Hound Club of America." The few changes between these two Standards consist of the word "perceptibly" instead of "sensibly" under head; the elimination of "i.e., pot-hooked" under tail (although we still see these in the show ring today) and, under forelegs, the Basset Hound Club of America used "crook'd" knee rather than "crooked knee." Perhaps this is where

Ch. Siefenjagenheim Lazy Bones won his first Specialty at the Basset Hound Club of California, 1956, and was handled by Frank Hardy, owned by Chris Teeter.

the English and American language differ, as Webster describes "crook'd" as having a crook and "crooked" as being askew.

From time to time other words were added or deleted, but nothing that changed the original Standard and the points of the smooth Basset Hound remained the same until the new Standard went into effect nearly thirty years later. Ch. Walhampton Andrew stood as the breed's ideal for all this time and was pictured in every edition until replaced with a photo of Ch. Siefenjagenheim Lazy Bones.

POPULARITY, PROBLEMS AND CHANGES

With the popularity of the Basset Hound came new problems to be dealt with. Questions arose by both breeders and judges, and it was time to evaluate the Standard—especially the possibility of disqualifications. An officer of the American Kennel Club had already advised me that the words "should disqualify" were not the same as "does disqualify," and there were numerous hounds being shown who were knuckled. We were also seeing a good number of long-haired Bassets, some stripped out and others shown in natural coat. The final straw was a phone call to this author from the American Kennel Club asking what I knew about long-haired Bassets. A letter had been received by them from a gentleman who was to do Sweepstakes at a Specialty, and he was asking how to handle this problem as there was nothing in the Standard to clarify. Two weeks later, armed with folders, articles, pedigrees and photos, I attended a meeting at 51 Madison Avenue and things moved rapidly from there on.

At a board of directors meeting of the Basset Hound Club of America, held at the home of President Paul Kulp, a new committee was formed to look into revamping the Standard. It consisted of: Margaret S. Walton, chairperson; Richard Basset, West Coast; Effie Seitz, Midwest; Walter Brandt, East Coast.

This group worked together extremely well and the present Standard was the outcome with a few changes proposed by the American Kennel Club. They had asked that certain things be added, such as dewclaws may be removed, tail is not to be docked, etc. The membership of the Basset Hound Club of America had already voted to accept the Standard, and with the additions in place, it went into effect in 1964 and has stood unchanged since that time.

THE OFFICIAL STANDARD
FOR THE BASSET HOUND

GENERAL APPEARANCE—The Basset Hound possesses in marked degree those characteristics which equip it admirably to follow a trail over and through difficult terrain. It is a short-legged dog, heavier in bone, size considered, than any other breed of dog, and while its movement is deliberate, it is in no sense clumsy. In temperament is mild, never sharp or timid. It is capable of great endurance in the field and is extreme in its devotion.

Ch. Xaviera of Cotton Hill
Bred and owned by Elizabeth Redmond
Shown by Joy Brewster, "Holly" finished her championship in 12 shows.
She is sired by Ch. Lyn Mar Acres Extra Man ex Ch. Christine of Cotton Hill.

Ch. Lyn Mar Acres Extra Man by Ch. Lyn Mar Acres End Man ex Tantivy Demon, a double daughter of Ch. Tomo. Bred by Margaret S. Walton and Jane Luce; owned by M. S. Walton.

ANALYSIS—This paragraph needs little explanation as it tells you exactly what to expect from the breed. It is a hunting hound, short-legged, heavy bone—and one must always remember the operative words here are SIZE CONSIDERED. Judges should not think that because of the wording ''heavier in bone'' that the hound must have as much as a Saint Bernard or a Mastiff. The word ''clumsy'' means exactly that, and one will find that a straight shoulder, lack of sternum and front legs set too far forward will make a hound ''clumsy.'' If, on a loose lead, the hound stumbles over nothing, you may be sure it would never make it in the field for any length of time. The Basset can be extremely temperamental and prefers to go its own way and do its own thing. It has always been a *mild*-tempered hound and has only become sharp in the last couple of decades when exhibitors were not satisfied to show the proper temperament and wanted show dogs to the point of aggressiveness. I well remember a prominent handler being badly bitten by his charge. The same goes for timid dogs with the tail between the legs and

Ch. OrangePark Grover went Best in Show handled by Elaine Rigden. All Santana-Mandeville breeding, having been sired by Ch. S-M Ichabod ex Ch. S-M Minnie, bred and owned by Mr. and Mrs. R. Wilton Meyer of California.

totally terrified. A reticent hound on any given morning is normal— 8 A.M. judging, wet grass or a stranger on the end of the lead will give you the ''I don't care'' attitude.

HEAD—The head is large and well proportioned. Its length from occiput to muzzle is greater than the width at the brow. In overall appearance the head is of medium width. The skull is well domed, showing a pronounced occipital protuberance. A broad flat skull is a fault. The length from nose to stop is approximately the length from stop to occiput. The sides are flat and free from cheek bumps. Viewed in profile the top lines of the muzzle and skull are straight and lie in parallel planes, with a moderately defined stop. The skin over the whole of the head is loose, falling in distinct wrinkles over the brow when the head is lowered. A dry head and tight skin are faults.

ANALYSIS—It was at this time that the American Kennel Club decided that in any new Standard there should be no reference made to any other breed. For eons the Basset had always been known to have a "Bloodhound head," and the committee found it extremely difficult to come up with just the right wording. It seems rather obvious that today very few new people both in the breed and judging it know what a "pronounced occipital protuberance" really is. Further we have those showing in the ring who seem to think "wrinkles over the brow" means bringing the "shawl" (which, in some bloodlines lies over the shoulder and has nothing to do with the head) up over the dome to give the hound "wrinkles." Many years ago I had a wonderful conversation with Mrs. Dodge, the grande dame of the famous Morris and Essex extravaganza and great Bloodhound breeder and exhibitor. She had asked to see a bitch I was showing at the time whose head had been raved about by a certain friend of hers. Before I honored her request I asked if she would describe a proper Bloodhound head, and her words were "Two wrinkles over the brow and a fold on either cheek." A size 9 lady in a size 44 dress does not make an attractive picture—neither does a Basset with loose hide falling off the wrong places.

THE MUZZLE is deep, heavy and free from snipiness. The nose is darkly pigmented, preferably black, with large, wide-open nostrils. A deep liver-colored nose conforming to the coloring of the head is permissible but not desirable.

ANALYSIS—Moderation in all things is a good rule to follow, even in breeding dogs. Too heavy and deep a muzzle gives a hound an "out of balance" look, and certainly snipiness, with just enough lip to cover the teeth, is equally unattractive. The large wide-open nostrils are essential for hunting. At the time this Standard was being prepared we had quite a number of breeders of red and white Bassets with light noses. In order to have a new Standard, concessions were made.

> THE TEETH are large, sound and regular, meeting in either a scissors or an even bite. A bite either overshot or undershot is a serious fault.

ANALYSIS—I will go on record here and state that I believe a bad mouth should be a disqualification. Unfortunately, at the time the Standard was written, in 1964, a number of bad mouths were being shown and winning and some were even being fixed. Only by keeping this serious fault out of the ring and out of your bloodline will we cease to see it.

> THE LIPS are darkly pigmented and are pendulous, falling squarely in front and, toward the back, in loose hanging flews. The dewlap is very pronounced. The neck is powerful, of good length and well arched.

ANALYSIS—The above is self-explanatory, for most hounds conform in foreface and lips as described. Occasionally one finds a hound with very little if any dewlap, but this is rare in a loose-skinned breed. A Basset with a short neck that does not "flow" into the shoulder is not a pretty picture; a beautiful head set on a well-arched neck of good length is. An interesting story comes to mind here, for when a club member read "well arched," she called me from the West Coast and informed me she had never seen a Basset with an arched neck. I simply asked her when she had ever seen a bull or a stallion *or most dogs* without an arch to the neck? She backed off rather quickly at this and admitted she perhaps was wrong, but that her hounds were not built that way!

> THE EYES are soft, sad, and slightly sunken, showing a prominent haw, and in color are brown, dark brown preferred. A somewhat lighter-colored eye conforming to the general coloring of the dog is acceptable but not desirable. Very light or protruding eyes are faults. THE EARS are extremely long, low set, and when drawn forward, fold well over the end of the nose. They are

velvety in texture, hanging in loose folds with the ends curling slightly inward. They are set far back on the head at the base of the skull and, in repose, appear to be set on the neck. A high set or flat ear is a serious fault.

ANALYSIS—Here we must differentiate between the eye being "slightly sunken, showing a prominent haw," and haw-eyedness or ectropion. Ectropion appears as a loosening and/or sagging of the lower eyelids, primarily at the centers. Unfortunately this exaggerated condition will gather all sorts of debris and cause great problems; the only solution for ectropion is surgical correction, which will disqualify the dog from the show ring.

While many owners think that the longer ear, extending *well* beyond the nose, is an attractive feature in their hound, that great length can be a detriment. A properly hung ear, low on the head and long enough to reach the end of the nose, is in much better balance.

FOREQUARTERS—The chest is deep and full with prominent sternum showing clearly in front of the legs. The shoulders and elbows are set close against the sides of the chest. The distance from the deepest point of the chest to the ground, while it must be adequate to allow free movement when working in the field, is not to be more than one-third the total height at the withers of an adult Basset. The shoulders are well laid back and powerful. Steepness in shoulder, fiddle fronts and elbows that are out is a serious fault.

ANALYSIS—The Basset has long been known as an "unbalanced, balanced hound," and it is principally because of the front assembly. Like its cousin, the Dachshund, the weight is borne on the front because of the manner in which it works in the field. While the Dachshund goes to ground, the Basset uses its sternum and powerful shoulders to go *under* brush rather than over, as do the larger working hounds. The sternum is not just a blob of fat covered with skin as some seem to think but is a properly shaped structure of bone and cartilage extending well back under the hound's body and *not*

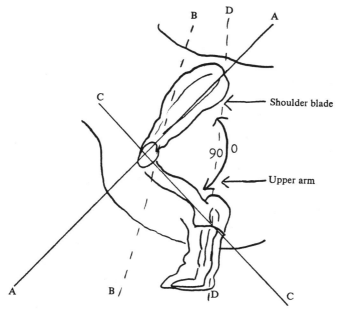

A. Solid line shows 45 degree angle of shoulder blade to ground level, allowing good reach of foreleg.

B. Dotted line shows steep shoulder blade placement and how it limits the reach of front leg. Incorrect.

C. Solid line shows upper arm of correct length, angling back and down to create an angle of 90 degrees between it and shoulder blade.

D. Dotted line shows plumb line from withers to back of heel, the best position to pose front to determine true angulation. Short upper arm would not permit foreleg to stand under withers and cover deepest part of chest, maintaining good balance.

Drawing of correct shoulder angles.

stopping between the front legs. The Basset uses the sternum much as a sled does its runners and it is therefore an absolute necessity. The shoulders are *well laid back*. How many breeders and judges today know how to measure a well-laid-back shoulder? Steepness in shoulder is a *serious fault*, yet how many of our Group and Best in Show winners have a well-laid-back shoulder?

THE FORELEGS are short, powerful, heavy in bone, with wrinkled skin. Knuckling over of the front legs is a disqualification. The paw is massive, very heavy with tough, heavy pads, well rounded and with both feet inclined equally a trifle outward, balancing the width of the

47

shoulders. Feet down at the pastern are a serious fault. The toes are neither pinched together nor splayed, with the weight of the forepart of the body borne evenly on each. The dewclaws may be removed.

ANALYSIS—Although knuckling over is a disqualification, it can, and has been concealed by an abnormal amount of wrinkled skin. Feet and legs on a hound are extremely important as is the toughness of the pads and the makeup of the paw. Please note that the wording is "*both* feet inclined equally a trifle outward"—it does *not* say one foot goes north while the other goes west. Unfortunately, it says "balancing the width of the shoulders"; I say unfortunately, for with wide, straight shoulders this can only mean that the front is also wide, giving one the impression that the hound moves with a waddling gait like a duck out of water.

BODY—The rib structure is long, smooth and extends well back. The ribs are well sprung, allowing adequate room for heart and lungs. Flatsidedness and flanged ribs are faults. The topline is straight, level and free from any tendency to sag or roach, which are faults.

ANALYSIS—Certainly the above description tells one exactly what the body is to be. It does *not* say that the Basset has a short back, long loin *or* a topline that either rises over the loin or drops off, giving the hound a low tail set. *The long rib cage and short loin give support to the vertebrae*; a short rib cage and long loin allow for disk problems because of the lack of support to the spine. Flanged ribs are found more often in short-backed Bassets and rarely in the longer body.

HINDQUARTERS—The hindquarters are very full and well rounded, and are approximately equal to the shoulders in width. They must not appear slack or light in relation to the overall depth of the body. The dog stands firmly on its hind legs showing a well-let-down stifle with no tendency toward a crouching stance. Viewed from behind, the hind legs are parallel, with hocks turning neither in nor out. Cowhocks or bowed legs are serious

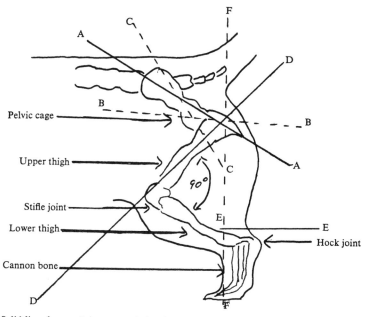

A. Solid line shows pelvic cage angled at 30 degrees to ground.
B. Dotted line shows flat pelvis, which would pull up upper thigh, and result in straight stifle; unless bones are very short, this gives a stiff stilted gait.
C. Dotted line shows steep pelvis, low tail set resulting, and lack of follow-through when moving.
D. Upper thigh of correct length which angles at 45 degrees to ground level, creating a 90 degree angle between it and lower thigh and almost the same between it and pelvis.
E. Correct length of lower thigh. If either thigh were shorter, on the same size dog, they would be straighter in order to meet. This would result in short gait or a straight stifle.
F. Dotted line shows best position to pose the rear to find angulation.

Drawing of correct rear angles.

faults. The hind feet point straight ahead. Steep, poorly angulated hindquarters are a serious fault. The dewclaws, if any, may be removed.

ANALYSIS—The first sentence in the above can very easily be misinterpreted if one does not take the time to realize that they have already been informed in the Standard that the shoulders must be well laid back, which does *not* mean *wide*; if the hindquarters then are the same width as the shoulder, they too are *not wide*, but rather nicely rounded and full of muscle. Earlier Standards describe the rear as ''round as an apple'' and a ''good hound to follow.'' There is one fault which has become evident since this Standard was written. We are seeing more "spraddle-reared" Bassets, which, in the earlier days, were never in evidence. This is where the moving hound goes wider with speed rather than the hind legs going toward the center line for balance.

> TAIL—The tail is not to be docked, and is set in continuation of the spine with but slight curvature, and carried gaily in hound fashion. The hair on the underside of the tail is coarse.

ANALYSIS—Over the years the tail on the Basset seems to have been straightened from the early Standards asking for a "teapot" tail until the present with only a slight curvature, which is correct for most hounds and certainly makes a more attractive picture. You may notice there is no mention of a white tip on the tail. Although this is useful in the field to keep track of the hounds, it is not a necessity. Some hounds have solid color and this would never be held against the dog in the show ring.

> SIZE—The height should not exceed 14 inches. Height over 15 inches at the highest point of the shoulder blade is a disqualification.

ANALYSIS—While working on this Standard, monthly trips were made to the A.K.C. One of the things that was suggested was that we make the height 16 inches maximum. The committee was slightly aghast for two reasons: first, the word "Basset" means low set—not 16 inches, and the other being that the hound would become long-legged, just what we were trying to avoid. The point was won and we compromised on 15 inches with 14 being the ideal "top." Most Bassets never attain even this height. Shortly after this Standard was adopted I watched a judge measure out two male Bassets, both being 16 inches and more; I breathed a sigh of relief for Bassets everywhere.

> GAIT—The Basset Hound moves in a smooth, powerful and effortless manner. Being a scenting dog with short legs, it holds its nose low to the ground. Its gait is abso-

Ch. Nancy Evans Fair Exchange
Sired by Ch. Sir Tomo of Glenhaven ex Eleandon's Happy Times. Bred by
Mona Ball. Owners: Nancy Evans & Georgia White. "Rosie" has the distinction of winning her championship in 2½ days with three 5 point wins from
the Novice class.

lutely true with perfect coordination between the front
and hind legs, and it moves in a straight line with hind
feet following in line with the front feet, the hocks well
bent with no stiffness of action. The front legs do not
paddle, weave or overlap, and the elbows must lie close
to the body. Going away, the hind legs are parallel.

ANALYSIS—Movement plays a very important part in both the
field and show life of the Basset Hound. At no time does the hound
exhibit a clumsy, plodding, rolling, bouncing gait. The dog moves
forward effortlessly and, with the correct anatomy, has the ability
to keep up with most other hounds in the Group as well as in the
field.

COAT—The coat is hard, smooth and short, with sufficient density to be of use in all weather. The skin is loose
and elastic. A distinctly long coat is a disqualification.

51

Ch. Tallyrand Keene has the distinction of having been named by virtue of having won Best Puppy in Show at a Hound Show at 5 months of age. Bred and owned by Robert and Kathryn Ellenberger and shown by Bob, they stated that the Hound Show judge was so "keene" on the puppy, that had to be the dog's name. Sired by Ch. Abbot Run Valley Prankster ex Ch. Talleyrand's Relue Annie.

ANALYSIS—Coat is quite often the result of proper care and nutrition and, although the hound may carry an undercoat in winter, it can still be hard, smooth and short. A long-haired Basset is very easy to spot and leaves nothing to the imagination. I have been asked to look at several longhairs and can assure you they would have been the envy of any long-haired Dachshund. With coat flowing to the ground, and beautiful feathering on the ears and legs, they were indeed very pretty. There were long coats in two particular bloodlines, and when crossed, never failed to produce the coat. This seems to have been virtually eliminated due to the fact that a long coat is a disqualification.

COLOR—Any recognized hound color is acceptable and the distribution of color and markings is of no importance.

ANALYSIS—Hound colors range from the blanketed hound, either black or red with white running gear, collar, blaze and tail tip; to splash markings, open or pied. Red and white can run from deep mahogany to orange or lemon. I have even seen solid black and tan hounds with only a few white hairs and wondered at the time if they reverted back to the French Basset Ardennais. From time to time one gets a "broken ear" in the litter and I have always found them very attractive and interesting. The markings on the ear are broken with white hairs and occasionally white patches. Pack hounds have much more symmetry of markings than show dogs as most breeders look for the best puppy in the litter regardless of color or markings. In judging packs, the hounds must be as near to the same height, weight, conformation and *color* as possible.

DISQUALIFICATIONS—Height of more than 15 inches at the highest point of the shoulder blade.

Knuckled-over front legs.

Distinctly long coat.

Approved January 14, 1964

ANALYSIS—These three disqualifications were the greatest problems in the breed in the 1950s and 1960s. At that time hounds were used more in the field and thus had good shoulders and rears with little problem in movement. As stated earlier, judges and breeders alike began asking what to do when these problems were viewed in the ring. Fortunately for the breed these three have been virtually eliminated from the show ring except for a rare case or two.

Now the breeders must work on other problems that have arisen because of the tremendous popularity of the breed, and judges must learn to reread their Standards in order to put up the best Basset Hound in accordance with the written Standard.

It is here I wish to add some personal comments on both breeding and judging. With great sadness I note how few judges really know the Standard and apply it in the ring. Today we have entirely too many Bassets with straight shoulders, no sternum and mismatched fronts, all of whom are winning. Judges either do not know or care that these are extremely serious faults in any hound bred for the specific purpose of hunting. Whether the Basset is used in the field is the owner's prerogative, but the fact is that it must represent the Standard as written and be able to do the job for which it was bred.

One cannot totally blame the judges, however, when breeders are content to breed and exhibit hounds with the above faults. How many of these breeders have walked a Field Trial, hunted with a Basset pack or attended hound shows where the Basset is doing what it was bred for? I wonder if any of these breeders producing upright shoulders have tried riding a straight-shouldered horse—if so they then should be able to relate to the pounding the front end takes whether it be horse or hound. Just be prepared to eat dinner standing up!

3

The Basset Hound in Art and Literature

My hounds are bred out of the Apartan kind,
So flew'd, so sanded, and their heads are hung
With ears that sweep away the morning dew;
Crook-knee'd and dew-lapp'd like Thessalian bulls;
Slow in pursuit, but match'd in mouth like bells;
Each under each.

A Midsummer Night's Dream, Act IV, Scene I

FOR MANY YEARS now it has been thought these lines from Shakespeare referred to the Basset Hound. Whether true or not, it certainly fits the breed, and as long as there seems to be no contest, they are a welcome addition to the breed's heritage.

As the breed progressed in France both authors and artists took to it and we find mention of it in many books as well as sculpture. In the mid-1800s the prominent artist Charles Oliver dePenne (1831–1897) apparently had a great love for the breed and included

Portrait of three Bassets by dePenne

Portrait *Chasse au Ferret*

it in a number of his paintings and watercolors. There are three known pieces of dePenne's Bassets in this country and perhaps others which have not come to light at this writing. The earliest known piece of his work is of three unknown French Bassets, one black and tan—Basset Ardennais—and two tri's with very plain heads and fiddle fronts—Basset d'Artois. A later watercolor entitled *Chasse au Ferret* shows five sportsmen with the ferret at hole, and in the background a gamekeeper with a hare over his shoulder, followed by two rather nice Bassets at heel. DePenne's third piece of work pictured two couples of Bassets *Tristan and Tristeuse, Temporal and La Tentatrice*, which was depicted on the cover of *The Chronicle of the Horse* a number of years ago and which was reproduced on china plates by Helen Boutell with the kind permission of the *Chronicle.*

About 1880 the English sculptor Albert Joy, R.H.A., did a delightful bronze of a Walhampton bitch nursing a litter of three puppies. Although a thorough search has been made, the identity of the model has never come to light. Mr. Joy exhibited in London

Bronze Basset with puppies—Albert Joy

from 1866 to 1893, and had 115 exhibits at the Royal Academy. This model measures 8½ inches at the widest width of the base and is 6 inches high.

In July of 1970 we received a letter from Gerald Massey of London, England, offering us the original clay sculpture of Everett Millais model of a typical Basset Hound, signed in monogram and dated 1888, which was exhibited in the First Summer Exhibition of that year at the New Gallery, Regent Street, London. To quote from the late Mr. Massey's letter: "The model is life-size: Height at shoulders, 12½ inches. Length from nose to set-on of flag, 34 inches. Tip of tail, which is well curved over the back to base, 23½ inches. The base, also in clay, is 26½ by 11¾ inches, and 2 inches thick. Painted all over a neutral terra-cotta colour, it is in very fine condition, but the base of the tail is showing a certain amount of cracking in the clay at the set-on."

Douglas Appleton's *The Basset Hound Handbook* (1960) reproduces somewhat poorly the front view of this model, stating it was a bronze. However, he has informed me he never saw the actual model, and was only told it was bronze. The photograph certainly shows a clay rather than a bronze medium, and of course a clay model would have to be sculptured first before a bronze could be cast. This fact is substantiated by an article in the *Kennel Gazette*, May 1888, regarding the "life-giving clay" model that Everett Millais exhibited as a "typical Bassethound." Naturally, we were both excited to have this piece of Basset history offered to us, but slowly and sadly we came to the realization that there were other things here to consider. In Mr. Massey's second letter he related how very carefully it would have to be crated and shipped. Realizing airlines are not always careful when handling bags, much less a valuable antique, and taking into consideration it was life-size and

Six couple of Basset Hounds resting in a kennel, by Valentine Thomas Garland 1884–1903. Oil on canvas, signed and dated 1894, 16″ × 22″. This was expected to realise $3,000/4,000 at Christie's Scotland on April 30, 1986 in a sale of English, Continental and Sporting pictures.

Bronze Basset by Bayre

would be difficult to protect with house dogs rambling around, we finally decided against the purchase. We hope that today it is in a museum or being appreciated by a private owner.

LOCATING BASSET ART

Over the years I have found the best way to locate books and prints on the breed is to follow the path of least resistance. Like most things, when you are desperately hunting for the impossible it is just not there! Books have turned up in some very improbable places, as have prints, paintings and etchings.

Antique shows and auctions are great fun and often sources of information even if nothing is available that day. Flea markets and second-hand stores may turn up prizes beyond your expectations, and if you make your wants known, there just may be something interesting back at the shop or under the counter. At one local antique show we found a small Britannia-ware Basset with a pincushion in his back. At another we found a "Cleo" bank—admittedly, it was not an antique but it certainly is a memento of the rapid growth of

Bronze Basset by Bayre

the breed stimulated by both Morgan and Cleo of TV fame. There was even a Little Golden Book done of Cleo that sold for twenty-five cents in 1957!

Often a very fine piece of American sculpture comes out and if you are an inveterate collector you will strain the groaning budget to add it to your already growing collection.

In the 1950s the noted sculptor Edward Marshall Boehm did a Basset puppy that sold for about thirty-five dollars and was a welcome addition for anyone in dogs. Today it has been appraised in four figures. An interesting side note is that friends have an unglazed figure of this puppy, which was left behind, untouched, when their house was robbed!

One of the later fine collectibles is the pair of Bassets—dog and bitch—done by Charles Di Gioia, comissioned by Finn Bergishagen and Knox Williams. Available at the time either singly or in pairs, and done in "Marblester" (powdered marble dust and polyester plastic resin), 165 pairs were made. Also done were seven pairs in bronze, and were numbered. These are excellent examples of the Basset and were done from life models.

From England came a charming etching of a puppy, done by Hug, in a limited edition of 265. It was done some time ago but perhaps a search of art galleries in large cities may turn up one of these, or even still older prints.

For those who own the English Beswick Basset on a wood base from 1967, she was Eng. Ch. Fochno Trinket, owned by Wendy Jagger and the cover girl on George Johnston's book *The Basset Hound* (1968). The modeler who created the statue was Mr. Gradington.

It is interesting how things come to the fore when you are least expecting them. My cousin breeds and judges Arabian horses, and while attending a seminar in Virginia, saw an early Basset bronze displayed among the horse models. She took the dealer's card and called me. I followed up on this lead to find he not only had the standing model by Antoine-Louis Bayre (1796–1875), but also a sitting model. Needless to say he very quickly made a sale and said that I was the only person who had ever asked for a Basset. Although this man dealt only with horse items, all horse lovers have a favorite breed of dog and I thank the anonymous horse/hound lover who parted with these two.

THE BASSET IN BOOKS

The popularity of the Basset increased and at the turn of the century many British authors had included the breed in dog books. Henri de Bylandt wrote a very extravagant two-volume work on all known breeds, translated it into three languages, enhanced it with beautiful plates and published it in 1909. He covered six varieties of the Basset including the Griffon and breeds related to the Basset. They are a worthwhile addition to anyone's library, if the volumes can be found.

There have been many books of value to include the Basset over the years, but one of my very favorites is *Hunting Dogs*, by Bert Cobb. Plates in this book are attached only at the top of the page and these may be removed for framing if you wish. Not only does Mr. Cobb include many famous champion hounds and sporting dogs, but plate 5 is of Erastus T. Tefft's Bassets Runt and Pippin (Ch. Lavenham Pippin).

Clay model of a Basset Hound.

Another favorite is entitled *An Artist's Models*, by Cecil Aldin, with references and plates of King Edward VII's rough Bassets. It includes details of Mr. Aldin's two seasons with the Walhampton hounds while "the owner was in India hunting the Outy Hounds." His understanding of the breed is evident when he writes, "They are exceptionally handy little fellows to hunt if you don't try to 'lift' them, and have your whippers-in carrying whips, which are never, on any provocation, to be used. Such shy little hounds should never be touched with thong, a rate being always more than sufficient."

There have been many delightful small books written regarding the Basset and one of the best was written by the breed's own Eileen Schroeder. In it she tells of purchasing her first Basset, raising it and her first shows. It covers her trials and tribulations, all written with great humor and love of her chosen breed. Mrs. Schroeder became active in both the Basset Hound Club of America, becoming secretary of the club for three years, and in all-breed clubs. This book is entitled *Going to the Dogs*, with wonderfully funny illustrations by

Arnie Leven. Published in 1980, copies may still be available with a little searching.

Another amusing small book is entitled *Walter The Improbable Hound*, written by Fred Ayer, Jr. A biography of a Basset with ideas of his own and his life in the fast lane (U.S. Highway 1-A), it is illustrated by Erich Sokol, who did his sketches with all "Walters" in mind. Because it was published in 1958, it may take a bit of searching to find this one, but it is well worth the effort.

One of my very favorites is entitled *Boswell's Life of Boswell*, sketched and written by Evelyn Leavens, and published in 1958. Boswell was sold to Miss Leavens as a pet and companion, his breeders never dreaming he would become a celebrity, but that he did. This book of sketches was done at the height of Basset popularity and appeals to all ages.

From Charleston, South Carolina, came a book entitled *The Bishop's Basset*, by Jessie O'Connell Gibbs, and published in 1970. It is a small book of photographs with the text in rhyme, and gives a Basset's-eye view of growing up in a rectory.

For the children in the family with their first Basset puppy there are two books they would definitely enjoy. The first is entitled *Bascombe, The Fastest Hound Alive*, written by George J. W. Goodman, with pictures by Paul Galdone and published in 1958. It is the tale of a clever Basset and two rabbit friends, Herbert and Sam. The second book is *Claude the Dog*, a Christmas story, with words and pictures by Dick Gackenbach, and published in 1974. It is lovingly done with a message for young and old alike.

Over the years there have been many other books written, some serious reading and others in a lighter vein, but all are worth collecting. There are also bronze and porcelain pieces and even small memorabilia such as cigarette cards and stamps available for collecting; in the early 1950s Congress playing cards manufactured decks with a head study of Ch. Hartshead Pepper on them.

Just keep your eyes and ears open and your wallet slightly ajar!

4

The New Puppy—
Choice and Care

THE DECISION has finally been made on the breed
that is best for the family. You have attended dog shows, spoken
with a few breeders as well as a veterinarian or two and people who
own the breed, and you have chosen the Basset. Now to find the
breeder who has what you desire in the breed. It is hoped you have
written to the American Kennel Club *and* the secretary of the Basset
Hound Club of America for a list of breeders in your area. You may
also have had access to a regional Basset club as well as an all-breed
club that keeps a list of members who have this breed.

FINDING THE RIGHT PUPPY

It is advisable to call these breeders, explain your wishes and
feel free to ask questions about the breed, prior to even looking. If
you are happy with the answers you receive, make an appointment
to visit the breeder and see the adult hounds, even though puppies
may not be available at that time. It is best to visit several breeders

Basset Hound puppies and children—a happy combination.

before you decide on a specific puppy. If you feel pressured into buying immediately, move on as *a good breeder is more interested in the home the puppy will be going into* than making a sale.

Assuming you are looking for a pet and companion, the breeder will probably have a few questions for you:

1. Is the yard fenced?
2. How old are the children in the family?
3. Have you owned a dog before this?
4. If so, what breed?
5. Why do you wish the sex you have requested?

We have always preferred to place a bitch puppy in a home where there are small children, mainly because they are cleaner, easier to housebreak, more loving to the entire family and usually show no favorites. This is not to say males do not make wonderful pets, but they are even more inclined to roam if not properly confined to the yard, are a little more difficult to house-train and usually extend their love to the female members of the family and merely accept the male members.

AGREEMENTS AND OBLIGATIONS

Once you have decided on *the* puppy, do not be surprised when the breeder tells you he/she is to go with American Kennel Club limited registration. This means that the Basset's offspring will not be eligible for registration. Along with this you may be asked to sign a spay/neuter agreement, which will state all pertinent information on the puppy including the reason for selling as a pet, i.e., turned front, steep shoulders, faults that would preclude it not being a show dog in the breeder's opinion. A good breeder has done this particular breeding for one reason—hopefully from this litter will come a top puppy to keep, and having selected that one, the rest of the litter will be nice, happy, healthy puppies, ready to make some family happy.

Along with the signed agreement, which has been carefully

read, you should be given a well-thought-out sheet of information. This will include details on:

1. Feeding
2. Number of feedings per day
3. Times, brand names and amounts
4. Worming dates with product used
5. All inoculations
6. The attending veterinarian's name and address

We have always asked that the puppy be vet-checked within seventy-two hours, with the findings reported back to us by the new veterinarian.

The puppy is now ready to depart on a new life and it is hoped you will have prepared thoroughly for the homecoming. A crate, either the airline type (Fiberglas) or open wire mesh, stands ready with either a bath towel or preferably a pseudo-lambskin pet bed in the crate. Either is easily washed and dried, keeping puppy warm and happy in a private hideaway. If the puppy is fed in the crate and has access to it for naps and nighttime sleeping, housebreaking will go very quickly if you take the pup out of doors immediately upon his/her awakening. Never allow your dog full run of the house until you are fairly sure mistakes will not be made.

Bitch with newborn puppies.

Bitch nursing week-old puppies.

Above all, do not allow puppy to climb stairs or go up or down more than two steps until about six months of age. With the heavy bone and anatomy of Basset fronts, great damage can be done by the dogs either pulling themselves up stairs or falling down them. Never pick up the puppy under the armpits or by the front legs— either scoop it up with both hands, supporting the entire body or carry the pup over your shoulder as you would a baby, with hands under the bottom. Do not allow the furniture to be jumped upon as this will result in a lifetime "couch potato." Bassets love to scratch and make a nest, and unless you are redecorating, the results on chairs and sofa can be disastrous.

Now that we have established territory and rules of the house, you will be pleased to enjoy the newest member of the family for the next twelve or more years.

There are always questions to be asked by the new owner prior to taking the new puppy home. These should be encouraged and readily answered by the breeder so that the change of homes should go as smoothly as possible for the puppy. As the breeder, be sure

Typical 8-week-old dog and bitch puppies.

your telephone number is on the agreement so that any question the new owners may have can be answered quickly and easily.

Occasionally a situation arises where there either may be an illness in the family or perhaps even an allergy to the puppy. The big question here is, will you take the puppy back? If you are dedicated to the welfare of the breed, this should be firmly stated when the new owner takes the puppy, as you want the best possible home for the youngster.

CRITICAL PERIODS

Most breeders know that there are five critical periods of a puppy's life and the first three apply while the puppy is in the care of the breeder. It is the breeder's responsibility to give the puppy the best possible start in life so that there will be few problems with the new owner in the months to come.

From eight through twelve weeks the puppy needs supervised human socialization and lots of love and security. At this point, the puppy has the ability to establish a permanent bond and a person-dog relationship, and is also capable of accepting gentle discipline. If the puppy remains with the breeder during this period, care must be given to socialize as much as is possible. If the puppy is sold during this period, this should be explained to the new owner, and care should be given that children and other animals in the new home not be allowed to frighten or hurt the puppy. Exposure to loud noises should be done gradually, and as most breeders have a radio and telephone near or in the whelping-puppy room, the youngster should be well acquainted with these. The pup should not be subjected to long walks or hard play with the children in the family without parental supervision.

From thirteen to sixteen weeks the puppy needs love, attention, discipline, socialization and security. A Basset may begin to emerge as a dominant personality, especially a male Basset puppy. At this age, a small amount of Obedience training could begin so that life will be easier for all concerned, but gentleness and much praise is *most* effective.

All of the above should be pointed out to those who wish to obtain an older Basset. While it is usually wise to take an older hound when you are looking for a top show dog, it does seem best to take a puppy from ten to twelve weeks if you want a loving house pet and companion, thus you are able to train in your own way and establish a rapport for the future.

LINES AND SUCH

Many new owners have heard the old wives' tales about "inbreeding, linebreeding and outcrossing" without ever understanding what these terms really mean. They raise important questions that should be answered in all honesty to the purchaser and explained fully as to why this breeding was done.

Ch. Ran-Su's Fanny Farmer was a daughter of Ch. Coventry Rock Andy (Ch. L.M.A. M'Lord Batuff ex a double daughter of Ch. The Ring's Ali Baba) ex Orangepark Gidget (Ch. Orangepark Dexter ex Ch. Margem Hills Ginger Fizz). Bred and owned by Susan Sutfin, Fanny was bred to Ch. L.M.A. Extra Man and again to Ch. Ran Su's Drummer Boy. Always keeping style and soundness in mind, Susan Sutfin did intense linebreeding and produced Ch. Ran-Su's Devon, Winners Bitch from the Bred by Exhibitor class at the 1991 BHCA National.

Inbreeding does not necessarily mean that the puppy will have horrendous problems or be schizophrenic; the very experienced breeder has merely tried to preserve the best of a bloodline by breeding father to daughter, littermates or mother to son. If nothing radical has resulted by twelve to sixteen weeks, the purchaser may be fairly sure they have a normal puppy. It must be remembered that inbreeding sets the bad characteristics as well as the good, and both are seen in abundance in inbred puppies.

Linebreeding is practiced by most breeders and this simply means that somewhere not too far back in the pedigree the sire and dam of the puppy will have some of the same ancestors. If these dogs were normal Bassets, there is no cause for the new owner to be alarmed, as this is most often the most dependable kind of breeding.

Outcrossing means that there are no related hounds in the first several generations of the pedigree and the puppy may or may not even look like the sire or dam but may indeed favor the grandparents or even great-grandparents.

THE NEW PUP AT HOME

The new owner should not hesitate to ask about the following:

1. Feeding as the pup gets older, i.e., when and how much more food should be given
2. Changes in diet
3. What weight the puppy should be at a certain age
4. Should the pup be given bones to chew on and if so, what kind

Most breeders are happy to hear from the new puppy owner from time to time and will gladly help with information in any way possible.

Grooming and Health Care

Grooming and bathing the Basset puppy is often asked by the new buyer and the answer is not always an easy one. A puppy being kept as a house dog will probably not get nearly as dirty or smelly as a hound kept out of doors or in the kennel. Basset puppies love to dig, and unless kept on concrete (which I decry), they will do so and have a wonderful time, thus becoming dirtier than the house puppy who is being walked on-lead or allowed onto the grass for exercise. I would not suggest bathing a puppy under twelve weeks, unless it becomes absolutely necessary, and then must be thoroughly dried and not allowed outdoors for several hours.

Ears and nails seem to be two problems for the new owner of a Basset. Ears should be checked every week and are very easy

A lovely 10-week-old puppy bitch.

A well-grown 7-month-old male puppy. This dog went on to become a top winner.

to keep clean by using a tissue wrapped around your index finger and wiping out the inside of the ear, making sure you *do not go too deep*. Cotton balls moistened with mineral oil are easy to use and get the surface dirt, although the inner ear should be dried following the use as oil tends to gather more dirt. Should there be very dark matter on the cotton or tissue, the puppy should be taken to the veterinarian to be checked as ear mites may be present.

Puppy's **nails** are easiest to keep under control if done on a regular schedule. It is best if you have help with one person holding and reassuring the puppy while the other nips the nail. If the nails are attended to regularly, they will not grow to great length and the puppy will enjoy the attention; should they be allowed to grow, you may have a major fight on your hands and a very frightened puppy who will resent the next session of nail clipping.

Spaying/neutering was heretofore normally done from six to nine months of age, but new procedures show that these operations may be done earlier in puppyhood and breeders are now looking favorably into this. Your new puppy may already have had the operation and will be spared the separation from breeder to new home to veterinarian and back to new home. This can sometimes be an upsetting experience for a young hound and with this new method it can be eliminated. The breeder will explain if this has been done and the new owner should receive the spay certificate.

The Multi-Pet Household

The breeder should always inquire if this is to be the only pet in the house or if there are other dogs or one or more cats.

Most Bassets love company and will get along very well with other breeds of dogs, but the new puppy should never be allowed to annoy or tease an older dog who is already the majordomo and knows it. A snarl or snap from the older one may result in not only putting puppy in its place but may give quite a shock, one never to be forgotten. A kitten or older cat seems to have an easier adjustment to a new puppy as they can almost always get out of the way if need be. Many breeders also have a cat or two around the house or kennel and puppy may have already been acquainted with this species, making it easy to adjust to a new friend.

All in all, Basset puppies adjust very well to a new home if given love, attention and proper supervision. Make your veterinarian your "best friend" and the breeder your "next best friend," and the puppy will be set for life—and a good one at that.

5

Care and Feeding
of the Basset Hound

THIS CHAPTER is being written because of re-
quests. My intent is not to try, in any way, to change your already
successful method of feeding.

Since the Basset Hound is such a complex breed, trying to
keep yours sound of leg and body should be of the utmost importance. Front structure and great bone must receive the proper balance
of food. The diet must never be overdone or unbalanced, or else
many unwanted problems will result.

Our hounds are fed a balanced kibble meal that is chicken-
based and contains no wheat or soy. We are firm believers in vitamin
E, so a 400 I.U. soft gel capsule is added to every dish regardless
of age; also one vitamin-mineral tablet. Added to this is a small
piece of *pork* liver, and over it all we pour beef broth, just enough
to moisten, as our hounds seem to prefer not to have their food soft.

We have fed pork liver for nearly forty years at the suggestion
of our veterinarian at that time, and research shows that, unlike beef
liver, it contains vitamin K. Whether this has had any effect over
generations I will not speculate, but I do know when our dogs have

been blood-tested, the reports have been negative. If I may quote from Dr. Collins's most enlightening book, *The Collins Guide to Dog Nutrition* (New York: Howell Book House, 1987) "While there may be some faction in liver as yet unidentified, one thing about liver is no mystery. It contains more nutrients in one package than any other natural food available to man or beast."

SUPPLEMENTS

As for vitamin E, a paper written by Dr. Wilfred Shute, the famous Canadian physician, well-known dog show judge and Doberman Pinscher breeder, gives us the following information: "Vitamin E deficiency affects the reproductive system (testicular degeneration, defective development of the embryo); the muscular system (skeletal muscular dystrophy, cardiac necrosis and fibrosis, etc.); the circulatory system (anemias); the skeletal system (incisor depigmentation); and the nervous system."

Dr. Shute goes on to give personal experiences with his own house dogs. "My wife's black Miniature Poodle was failing rapidly at the age of eleven. We took him to our summer cottage near Dorset and expected to have to bury him there. At my wife's suggestion, we started him on 200 international units of Vitamin E a day. He was soon well, acting like a six-month-old puppy, and lived six more years. Our six-year-old Doberman, Ch. Kaukauna's Gold Braide, was also started on Vitamin E, just because she was our other house dog. She regained her youthful bounce and lived a full and extended life."

We do not now, nor have we for years, fed calcium except when prescribed by the veterinarian for a specific reason, which has been rare over these past fifty years. Should you care to use nutritious additives such as cottage cheese, yogurt, scrambled egg or a bit of regular cheese to your dog's diet—fine; these will give you all the necessary calcium your friend needs without overdosing.

Bassets are well known for having such abnormalities as turned fronts, flanged ribs, peculiar rears, poor coats; many of these prob-

Ch. Lyn Mar Acres P. T. Barnum (Ch. L.M.A. Press Agent ex Topper's Wilhunt Judi—a daughter of Ch. L.M.A. Top Brass). Owned by Mr. and Mrs. Lefferts, he was returned to Lyn Mar Acres in his later life. This photo was taken at 10 years of age, excellent testimony to the good care and feeding he received throughout life.

lems are caused by improper nourishment or the lack of a balanced feeding program. Some people feel that pushing this or that produces greater bone. I will tell you now that bone is genetic, and while the Basset should have ample amount of bone, it is better to have a bit less and a sounder hound.

NURSING MOTHERS

If you intend to breed your bitch, she should have a thorough checkup by your attending veterinarian. Be sure her shots are up-to-date prior to her coming into season. Since proper nutrition begins with the dam, she can be kept on her regular diet for the first few weeks following breeding. As she progresses in size, she should receive not only more food but twice-per-day feedings. A few days prior to the due date she will probably get a bit fussy about her meals. It is at this time we give her what she likes; that is, mainly meat, liver, cottage cheese, yogurt, actually whatever she prefers. Our veterinarian has always maintained that a smaller puppy makes an easier delivery—a healthy puppy will gain weight very rapidly and make up its size.

After whelping, the bitch is given a light diet of beef broth or beef and rice, and then gradually they resume their regular diet with the usual addition of extras mentioned above. As the litter grows, the dam will consume more food, and more feedings are offered through the day. The number of feedings will depend entirely on how many puppies she is nursing—a recent litter of fifteen meant four feedings per day for mum, plus three times per day of supplemental bottle feedings for the puppies.

PUPPY FEEDING

While bottle feeding is time consuming I have always found it most rewarding. The puppies, because they are used to nursing their dam, seem to take immediately to the bottle with little or no coaxing. Occasionally one will balk at the nipple since it is not the same consistency as the dam's, but a few squirts of formula into the mouth and the pup grabs hold—if hungry.

When feeding a large litter I place the bitch on one side of me and the entire litter on the other. I then offer the bottle to each, and when the puppy is full, give it to the dam. There is usually no fussing from her, as a rest from a large crew is welcome. She may put her head on my lap and watch until the first babe drops off the bottle and is returned to her, but after the first few feedings she will settle down and usually take a nap.

There are several good puppy formulas on the market and we have used two of them satisfactorily over the years, but have usually returned to the old "tried and true" of:

1 can evaporated milk
1 can boiled water
2 egg yolks
1 cup plain yogurt

Place all ingredients in your blender and whirl a few seconds; pour through a very fine strainer and refrigerate. If it is not used in a twenty-four-hour period the dam will always help you out by devouring it.

I prefer to wean my puppies early, for, like all youngsters, they love to try something new. There are several good weaning formulas on the market in the form of fine meal to be mixed with warm water. Should you prefer to start them out on regular puppy meal, and they seem too young to properly chew some without great effort, try grinding it in your blender or food processor to make a fine meal. To this you may add some formula, yogurt or cottage cheese, all of which they love. We also add a tablespoon of "liver guck" to one feeding; this is the coagulated blood and bits of liver plus broth that has been slightly simmered. We also mash a vitamin-mineral tablet into the feeding—the number per day depends entirely on how many puppies are being fed. When weaning early we give six feedings per day with the dam doing night duty. Gradually this is dropped to five, and by eight weeks of age they are on four feedings per day. By twelve weeks of age the pets are ready to go to their new homes and are still on four feedings; it is then up to the new owners and their veterinarian to decide the future.

Ch. Strathalbyn Shoot To Kill (Lyn Mar Acres Radar ex Tantivy Blond Sidonia), owned by J. J. J. McKenna, Jr. and Eric F. George (breeder). This dog is remarkable on two counts. He was one of the country's most outstanding pack hounds having been named Grand Champion at the Bryn Mawr Hound Show and garnered multiple Group wins and placements owing to both good breeding and good grooming. *Ashbey*

6

Grooming the Basset Hound

by Blackie and Howard Nygood

WELL-GROOMED Basset Hounds as pets or for show are a delight. They do not smell. They do not chew, scratch or lick themselves constantly. People who say, "Oh, but Basset Hounds smell bad," are people who do not know well-groomed Bassets.

STARTING WITH PUPPIES

Grooming starts with puppies. We start trimming nails, for example, at ten days and try to trim every ten days for the rest of the dog's life. "People" nail clippers are great for a puppy's tiny, thin nails. Just take off the tips, mainly to get them used to being held and manipulated. Cuddle them at the same time so it is always a pleasant association. As soon as they can stand fairly well (six weeks or so) start putting them up on a table, again to get them used to it and to prepare them for future sessions on a grooming table. Pose them briefly (believe us, it will be brief) and praise them. Keep these sessions short and sweet. After a while it will be second nature to them, and a table-trained Basset Hound, pet or show, is a joy to the human back.

Puppies can be bathed as early as eight weeks and should be exposed to a bath before going to their new homes. A baby bathtub or dishpan of warm water (stick your elbow in it) with a coffee measure of Lux or Ivory liquid hand dishwashing detergent is all that's needed. *In dilution* this will not hurt their eyes. Follow directions carefully on all regular dog shampoos if you use them, and the veterinarian's instructions to the letter with any medicinal shampoos. Pour the warm water over the puppy, talking reassuringly all the time. Make it quick, rinse thoroughly with warm water and dry well with towels and a hair dryer if needed. "Spot" baths (a messy rear end, or ears dragged through something) can be done the same way without total immersion.

TABLE TRAINING

When the pup gets older, train your dog to put front feet up on the grooming table. Pat your tummy so the dog jumps up on you, then swing the pup's front feet over to the edge of the table, and what's that in the middle of the table? A treat! As the dog reaches for the treat, boost up the rear end and the dog is on the table easily—and happily, too! Eventually the treat can be dispensed with, but some dogs continue to jump up at every grooming table they pass—just in case.

Get your dog used to a noose. A strong grooming bar on the table with a noose attached is a groomer's best friend. Nothing is more pathetic than to see a grown person pursuing a dog all over the table. Never mind the Poodle people with their trained-to-stay-on-top dogs. Many a Poodle has jumped off to break a leg or escape. Get your Basset Hound used to a noose. Life will be much easier for both of you.

As soon as a puppy is used to the table routine, begin with a light brushing, ear cleaning, eye cleaning and tooth check. These all get puppies familiarized with being handled and examined, making it infinitely easier for judges and veterinarians to go over them later. They develop confidence in themselves and start bonding with people—wonderful for temperaments.

For either pet or show the routine is the same with just a little extra "oomph" for the show dog. Start with a really thorough *brushing*. Use a slicker brush on a heavily shedding dog. A bristle brush, grooming mitt, fine tooth comb and shedding tool are great for cleaning out loose hair. Start behind the ears and brush, brush, brush. The amount of hair one Basset Hound can shed is amazing, but with every stroke you are not only removing dead hair but dirt as well. Do not bear down too hard so as to irritate the skin, and do not expect a Basset to stand for the entire process. You will hit its ticklish spot and the dog, no matter how old or well trained, will go into spasms of wiggles.

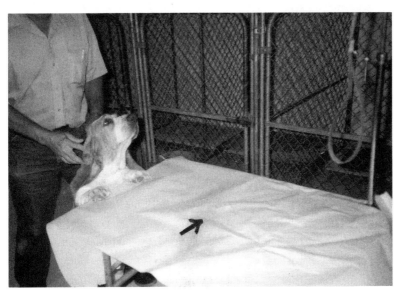

Training dog to put feet on table. Note dog biscuit on paper in middle of table and the ready grooming noose.

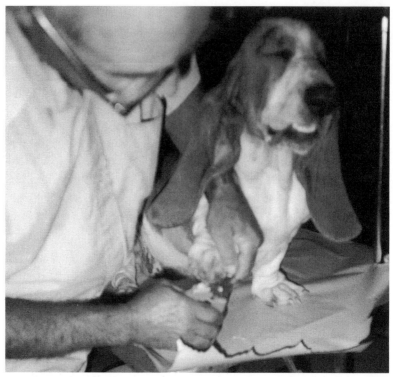

Cutting nails helps keep a dog's foot in shape and helps keep pasterns strong.

After getting as much hair out as possible, do *nails*. As these have been done religiously every ten days (well, nobody's perfect) they will not need extreme trimming. If you have a dog that absolutely hates the manicure bit, as we once did, try this: two people, one with clippers, one with dog biscuits. Start off by giving one biscuit per nail. The dog is so engrossed in the treat as to forget the feet. Gradually cut the treat to half, then just sort of let the dog gnaw on the treat while the nails are done. With a rapid flow of nonchalant chatter and an endless supply of treats, you can get such a dog to endure the clipping eventually with no trouble at all.

Use whatever type nail cutter you are used to or an electric grinder type if you know how to use it and the dog knows the sound and feel of it. We use a cutter and finish off the rough edges with a

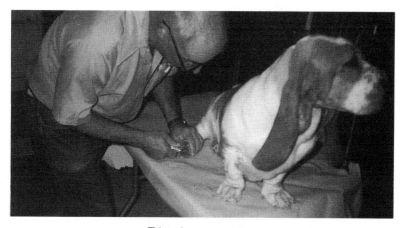

Trimming rear nails.

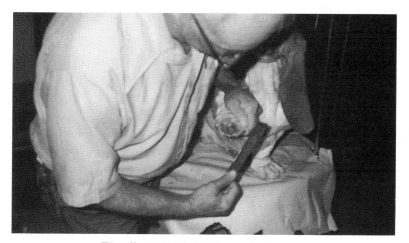

File off rough edges after trimming nails.

regular fine carpenter's file. If you cut a nail too close (this is usually in front of the new owner who thinks you have maimed the dog for life) take a pledget of cotton and press around the nail, or dip it in Kwik-Stop clotting powder. The bleeding will stop in a few minutes and be forgotten.

BATH TIME

With the coat brushed out and the nails done, start the water in the tub. A regular bathtub, *raised* on legs to *waist height*, is a godsend if you are bathing big dogs regularly. With the dog on the table, it is easy to lift it right into the tub. Have a spray attachment ready for rinsing, a pile of towels, and a leash to get the dog outside in hot weather or into a drying cage in cold. While the tub fills, clean eyes. We use a mixture of ¼ grain zinc sulfate to 1 ounce distilled water, made up at a pharmacy. Any human eye wash will do, or just plain warm water. Wet a cotton wad with the wash and gently wipe the eyes clear. Some dogs make up a lot of eye matter and some do not. If any eye problem persists, get the dog to your veterinarian.

Ears on a Basset Hound do not need to be a problem. More Basset odors can be traced to dirty ears than any other cause. Because they are long, air cannot get in to keep them dry as on a prick-eared dog. Oils, wax and dirt tend to build up. Some dogs' ears need cleaning every day, some every week. Again, familiarity with the process is your biggest help. Start young and they will never resent it. Take a wad of cotton, pour on some alcohol, and with the cotton wrapped around your finger, clean as deep as you comfortably can go. Some dogs will object all the time, others will never be bothered; but if they are, look into the ear to see if some problem has developed. Repeat the cleaning process until the cotton is no longer soiled with ear matter. If there is a musty smell, redness or other questionable condition, get the dog to a veterinarian for diagnosis and treatment. As with eyes, regular care is the best prevention of infection and trouble.

Now the tub is as full as you like. We prefer it almost to the dog's stomach. Put three or four coffee measures of the liquid hand dishwashing detergent in the water, and swish around gently to mix. Don't put it in before the tub is full or all you will get is suds. Put the dog in the tub and pour the warm water all over it. Rub to get down to the skin and if necessary use a bit of shampoo on extra dirty hocks, under the front legs and under the chin. The dogs love the rubbing and warm water massage. We had one

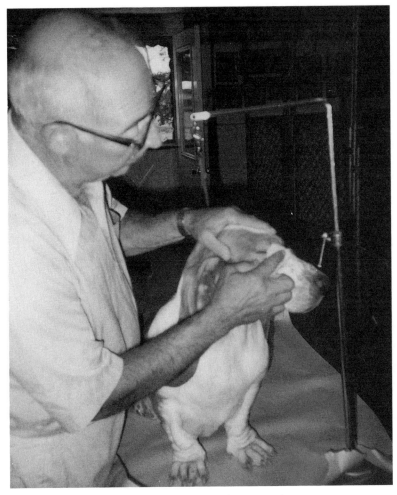

Cleaning the eyes with eye wash.

Basset who always fell asleep in the tub; we had to hold his head above water.

Drain the tub, still rubbing and chatting with the dog, rinse well with a spray particularly where extra shampoo was used and with a damp sponge extract as much water as possible. Then towel dry, lift out of the tub and dry either outside on hot days or with a dryer. A stand dryer or one attached to a wire cage makes it easy and saves time. Cover the cage with the towels used to dry (they'll

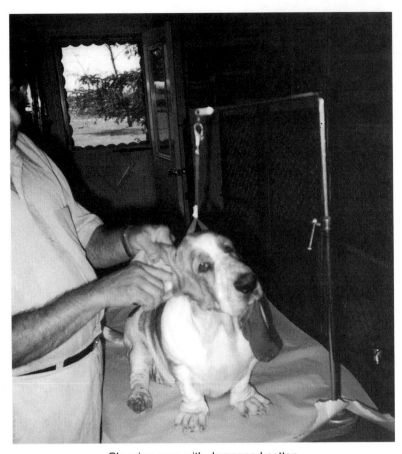

Cleaning ears with dampened cotton.

dry, too) and hook the dryer so it does not vibrate and travel away from the dog.

When the dog is dry, back onto the table for the finishing touches. The bath will probably have loosened more hair so a brushing will take care of that. Check the dog over, proclaim it is the best, cleanest, sweetest animal in the world, offer a treat and you're done!

SHOW GROOMING

The grooming of a Basset Hound for show should have started when its breeding was planned. The desirable Basset Hound coat—short, sleek, easy to care for—is to a large extent the result of genetics, not diet or care. These will maintain a good coat in show condition but they cannot make a poor coat better. A heavier coat is acceptable in winter and/or on dogs kenneled outside. Thick, furry undercoats are undesirable. A long coat similar to that of an Irish Setter is a show disqualification. While much may be done to "improve" a Basset's coat with clever trimming, it cannot change the genes that made it need trimming in the first place.

Trimming

Trimming is done to neaten up the appearance of the dog for the show ring. While many exhibitors simply run a towel over the dog and announce it ready, when push comes to shove the shining,

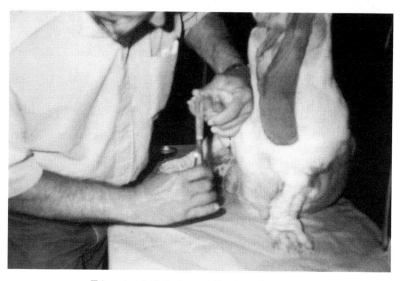

Trimming hair between the toes for show.

Trimming ridge of heavier hair on the neck for show.

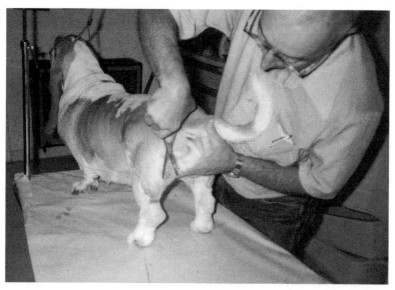

Trimming heavier hair on the thighs for show.

92

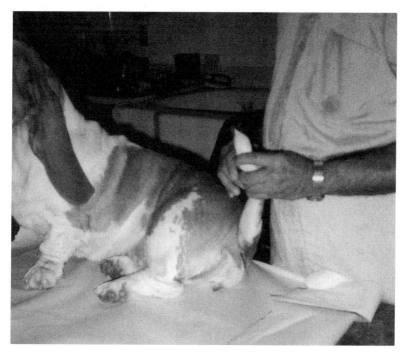

Tidying up the tip of the tail.

clear-eyed dog with the extra-cared-for look may have just the edge needed for the winning ribbon.

While the dog is on the grooming table, trim hair on the feet flush with pads and remove untidy hairs around toenails and between toes, giving the feet a neat appearance. If there is extra hair making ridges on the neck, trim these ridges carefully with thinning shears. *The idea is to neaten, not sculpt.* Some dogs have thicker hairs on the back of the thighs; these can be trimmed with thinning shears also.

Do not trim the brush (thick hair on underside of tail) but a tuft of hair at the tip of the tail can be trimmed. A Basset Hound is not a carved-out dog. What you see is what you get—but you can always help a little.

If you prefer a clean muzzle, trim the whiskers and eyebrows. This is purely a matter of choice. Be sure if you do trim to cover

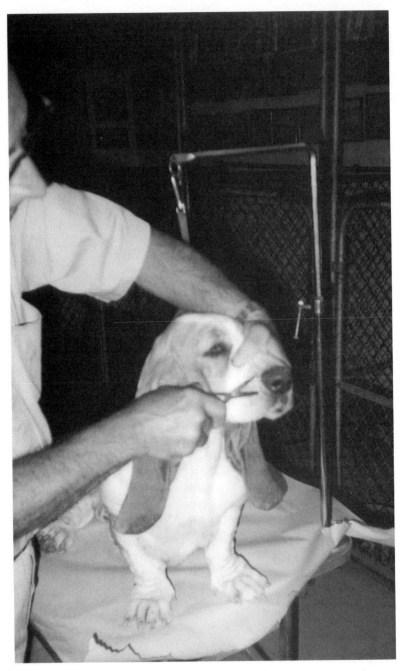

Trimming whiskers. Note the curved shears, rounded ends, pointed away from eyes.

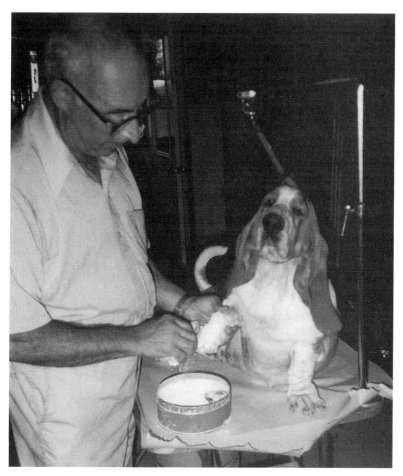
Chalking (1) Brushing chalk into dampened coat.

the dog's eyes with your other hand, to use rounded-tip shears and to hold the ends of the shears away from the dog's eyes. A sudden move could cause the shears to jab—better you than the dog.

SHOW TIME

On the day of the show, table the dog and brush again. Check eyes and ears (if your dog objects to the ear bit, skip it *at* the show,

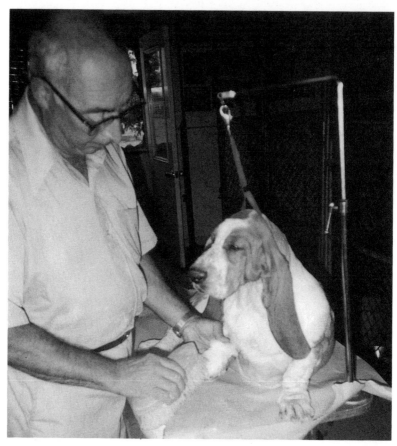

Chalking (2) Brushing out chalk.

as you do not want a lot of head-shaking in the ring). If necessary
(rainy day, mud puddle, crate accident on the way to the show) dip
a sponge in water and the good old dishwashing liquid and clean up
the area. Use a damp sponge to avoid excess wetting. Dry with a
towel and if needed pack white areas with grooming chalk. Dampen
the area first with a damp sponge and clear water, brush chalk in
thoroughly, let dry and brush out *all* chalk. *Any chalk remaining
can cause the judge to withhold all awards from your dog and get
you in big trouble with the AKC.* A good way to check is to brush,
then with a damp sponge, pat the area. Any white on the sponge
means further removal is needed. If this is the case, why chalk? It

Chalking (3) Patting out excess chalk with damp sponge.

brightens up yellowish coats and takes out any remaining dirt with it as you brush.

If the dog has a dry-looking nose, a pat of Vaseline rubbed on will shine it up.

Look over the whole animal. If your Basset is as handsome as can be, spray lightly with gloss spray, rub again and there's your show dog!

HELPFUL HINTS

1. To remove the last loose hairs, dampen your hands and, starting at the stop, rub toward the tail. Go over the whole dog this way and you'll be surprised at how much hair comes out. As your hands dry off, more hair is pulled.

2. If insects are bothering the dog at an outdoor show, spray lightly with insect repellent or flea and tick spray. The oily base will make the coat shine and it will help keep bugs away.

3. Anal sacs: It is good to check these from time to time, especially if you have seen the dog dragging the rear end or trying to chew at it. Table the dog and with a big wad of cotton, gently press on either side of the anus. If the glands are full, foul brown matter will be squeezed out on the cotton. Sacs can become infected and require medication. If the problem persists, get the dog to your veterinarian or have him/her clean the sacs in the first place if this just isn't your style.

4. Teeth: Cleaning teeth can be a big deal. Some people brush their dog's teeth every day. Some take them to the veterinarian to have them cleaned. Some dogs need anesthesia to have this done. We clean them at home on dogs that will tolerate it. Most do, being Basset Hounds and just assuming we know best. A regular dental tooth scraper will remove tartar and plaque. If done regularly, this will prevent many problems like foul breath and later expensive and uncomfortable dental procedures. You may be able to get a tooth scaler from your dentist.

BASIC GROOMING EQUIPMENT:

- Grooming table, table noose and/or overhead noose
- Slicker brush
- Grooming brush or mitt

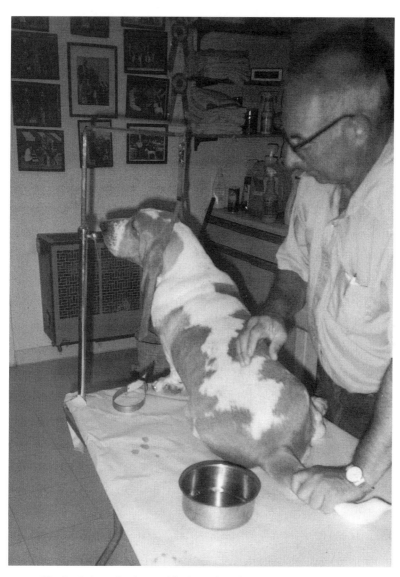

Final rubdown is done with damp hands to pull out loose hair.

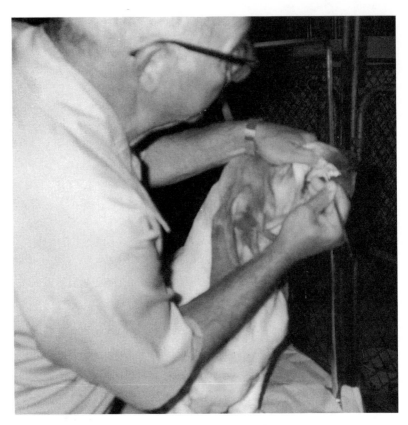

Cleaning teeth with a scaler.

- Shedding tool (Rake)
- Flea Comb
- Steel comb with 1-inch to 1½-inch teeth
- Nail clippers or grinder
- File, if clippers are used
- Cotton
- Kwik-Stop (Clotting powder)
- Alcohol
- Eye wash
- Towels
- Paper towels
- Lux or Ivory liquid hand dishwashing detergent and/or dog shampoo

100

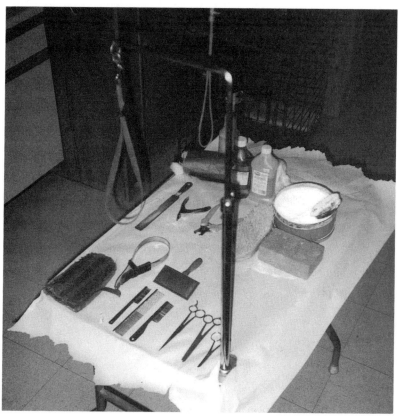

Grooming equipment
Table with an attached noose
Cord noose permanently in ceiling

Front: *L to R:* Grooming mitt
                Grooming tool
                Slicker brush
                X-fine flea comb
                Long tooth comb
                Flea comb
                Straight shear
                Thinning shear
                Whisker shear

Back: *L to R:* Nail file
               2 styles nail cutters
               Chalk brush
               Chalk sponge
               Chalk box
               Cotton
               Eyewash
               Alcohol

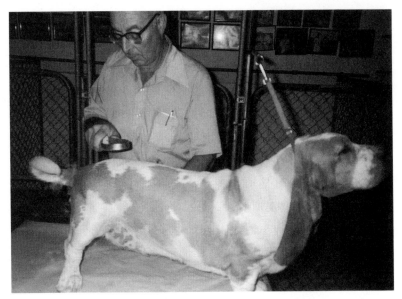

Use a shedding tool to remove loose hair.

Add for Shows:

- Small bristle brush for applying chalk, corn bristle/horse hair brush for removing chalk
- Grooming chalk
- Grooming dishes
- Gloss spray
- Rounded point shears for whiskers
- Straight shears
- Thinning shears
- Bug spray

Nice to Have:

- "Dry" dog shampoo or Pet-Wipes
- Antihistamine for swelling from insect bites
- Ice bag for same

7

Exhibiting Basset Hounds in Conformation

by Blackie and Howard Nygood

T O BE an exhibitor with a winning dog requires a good dog to begin with.

While the most artful handling job can make a mediocre dog look better, it cannot make it a better dog. Be sure the dog you have bred or bought is show quality. Do not give in to pressure from yourself or the breeder to finish it for the sake of the sire or dam. They don't care; the ego trip is for the owner or breeder. Know the dog's qualities and faults, and coldly, objectively decide. Get opinions from people not personally concerned, but not too many. Too many opinions are as bad as too few. Your dog is the same dog with or without Ch. in front of the name, and some of the biggest winners have been failures as producers and studs.

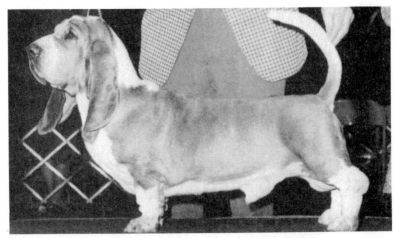

Ch. Slippery Hill Hudson (Studly von Happy Jack ex Slippery Hill Mocha), bred by Leonard Skolnick and owned by Mrs. Alan R. Robson. At that time his show record established him as the top winner in the breed.

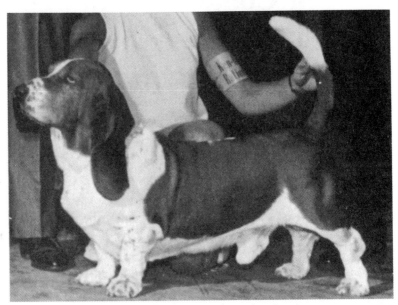

Ch. Musicland's Mountain Music was bred, owned and shown by Jeanne Dudley Hills of Musicland Kennels. Known for very sound hounds of good type, Jeanne Hills is still breeding and showing Bassets.

These two dogs show that a well-bred and competently shown Basset can win in any ring in any time period.

PREPARATION AND TRAINING

Having decided the dog is worth showing, start training. Assuming your new Basset is a puppy, begin as soon as your dog can walk fairly steadily. Even if yours turns out not to be a show dog, the dog should learn to walk on a leash. Slip a fabric lead on the dog's neck (an old soft Resco is great) and let the pup drag it around for a few minutes a day. Watch, as you don't want it to get tangled up.

After your Basset is used to the feel of the collar and lead, pick up the lead and walk wherever the pup wants to go. Talk and chirrup to the dog, gradually increasing the pressure on your end. Keep sessions short and fun. If the puppy balks at the slightest pressure, use a treat to cajole the pup along. Bend over, talk, sing, act like an idiot but keep that gentle pressure on until the puppy realizes going along with you is fun and the right thing to do.

Gradually increase the discipline and the praise when the dog does a good job. Do *not* yank or fight to hold the head up, or lose your temper. You can't even show at a match show until your pup is three months old, so what's your hurry?

Tables

Meanwhile, on a table, start practicing show posing. If any phase of Basset Hound training drives people nuts, this is it. You need five hands at least, what with front, rear, tail, head, sagging in the middle, sitting and the eternal "rear-leg-one-step-forward" ploy. Use a ribbed or other nonsmooth surfaced table; *keep it fun* even though you might want to wring the little darling's neck.

After your Basset learns posing on the table, try setting up on the ground, as Basset Hounds are no longer tabled at shows. Indoors, use a piece of old carpet as "matting" and practice in front of a mirror. *Watch the dog, not yourself.* Don't worry about the head and tail yet. Get the feet to stay put where you want them first.

Some judges will use a ramp to raise the dog for examination. If the dog is tabled trained, simply practice walking up a short incline and you'll have no problem.

A nice easy swinging gait, with the dog's head not too high nor too low, shows a Basset to best advantage.

Ring Practice

Now that your future champion will go nicely beside you on your left side, and will stand still (almost) when posed, start the refinements. Basset Hounds are scenting dogs and as such would normally move with their noses low to the ground. Very few judges,

106

however, will put up a dog shown in that manner. On the other hand, the super show dog (who would probably faint at the sight of a rabbit) who swings around with nose high in the air may look impressive but not like a Basset Hound. Find a happy medium that looks good for your dog and train it to move on a loose lead at that angle. Use bait or whatever gets the desired result.

When posing the dog, again hold the head at the most attractive level for that dog. You can string the dog up, that is, hold the head up with the lead, or hold the chin or flew, whatever is best for the dog and you. The Basset Hound Standard says, "The skin over the whole of the head is loose, falling in distinct wrinkles over the brow *when the head is lowered*." (Emphasis is ours.) Do not have your hound pointed skyward and then pull up the skin. It just looks wrong.

To acquaint your Basset with the ring, set up a "dummy" ring in your yard. Practice the common show patterns: up and back, the "T," the "L" and the triangle until you and your dog do them smoothly.

A good show pose with the dog stacked, and the head held by a lead.

SOCIALIZATION

Socialization is most important. Get your puppy out everywhere possible. Some stores will still allow dogs. Malls are great. Don't push the dog on people, just sit or walk around and let people and kids greet the puppy. You can ask them to go over it (pet it and feel its structure). If the puppy is shy or uncomfortable, don't force it. Bring it home and ask neighbors to come in and make friends. Get it used to a crate, a car, odd noises. If you can find a tent like a dog show tent, walk the puppy around it and under it so flapping and shade and ropes don't faze the dog at a show. If there is a local kennel club, take pups to the training classes most of them offer. Go on school visits with the puppy. The more experiences it has, the steadier show dog it will be.

When you and your dog are ready, take in a few match shows. These are "practice" dog shows, much like scrimmages. They are wonderful for schooling exhibitors, dogs and judges. They should not be taken as the "be all and end all," or as a career in themselves. Use them for socialization, schooling the dog and you, and they will be of great help.

READY, SET—GO TO SHOW

Before you enter your dog at the first real show, attend a couple to get a feel of things. Watch judging of other breeds as well as Bassets in order to get an idea of judging patterns and methods. Get on the various show superintendents' mailing lists for premium lists, which will tell you who is judging where and when. Ask the breeder which judges should like your dog's type. Judging is very subjective—one judge's Best of Breed is another one's fifth out of five.

First Things First

A show usually is entered around three weeks ahead. Mail in the entry blank found in the premium list. You will receive by return

Henry and Ann Jerman's Tal-E-Ho Kennels are known worldwide and have become the kennel behind much of the breeding in Denmark, Holland and on the Continent. Ch. Tal-E-Ho's Prancer was by Tal-E-Ho's George ex Tal-E-Ho's Ka-Ro.

mail your entry slip with dog's catalogue number and a judging program showing in which ring and at what time Basset Hounds will be judged.

Get a copy of the American Kennel Club Rules and Regulations for Registration and Dog Shows and read it cover to cover. When you sign the entry blank you are stating that you understand these rules. If you are going to show dogs you should know the rules, just like any other sport. Have an experienced exhibitor explain things like the point system, Reserve Winners and what a major is. It will save time and embarrassment when you enter the ring with your future champion.

In addition to your basic grooming tools, take a few creature comforts to the show. Take rain gear, boots, lunch for yourself (dog show food can be awful, and expensive). If possible do not feed your dog before a show and not at a show. A chair is nice. Take plenty of ice, and your own water for the dog and you. Take a paper bag for your trash. Baskets at shows can be few and far between, and you don't want to be a dog show slob.

For baiting the dog, boil beef liver in water with garlic powder, then dry it out in a slow oven on paper towels. Freeze in convenient-size packets. Or use whatever treat—cheese, hot dogs, biscuits, etc.—brings out the best in your dog.

One suggestion—gentlemen, always wear coat and tie, and ladies, never wear a long, flowing skirt that can hide the hound when gaiting. Good-looking, comfortable sportswear is always correct.

At the Show

Do as much grooming as possible at home and get to the show early so you are not rushed. You need time to unload, park, water and exercise your dog, groom it and crate it till judging time so your dog can relax. Watch the judge do the breeds ahead of Basset Hounds, if possible, to know the ring procedure. Get your dog to ringside, pick up your armband from the steward (the number is on the entry slip) and relax. If it is a hot day, keep your Basset in the shade with a wet towel to keep the dog as cool as possible. When you are in the ring, keep the dog under the tent or shaded with your body. Have your bait in your pocket, and a small cloth or Handiwipe to clean up drool or for a final polish.

In the Ring

In the ring remember you are showing *your dog*. Set up and move the dog to best advantage. Point out your dog's virtues subtly. Do not shove them in the judge's face. Watch professional handlers from ringside as they emphasize their dog's good points while ever so discreetly pulling apart the dog next to them. Watch and listen to the judge. Do as asked smoothly and promptly. Don't miss your calls and be scratching your nose when the judge is looking at toplines.

Chi Mi-Lin's Patton, bred and owned by Mr. and Mrs. Michael Sosne, sired by Ch. Tal-E-Ho's Top Banana ex Ch. Bayartois Amy. Patton became a very prominent show dog as well as a top sire.

Do not race around the ring with a Basset Hound. This may be fashionable and running dogs may win but it is wrong. The Basset was bred to hunt rabbits followed by people on *foot*. They were bred for stamina, endurance and "deliberate movement." The Oxford English Dictionary defines *deliberate* as "done of set purpose, studied; not hasty or rash." Some exhibitors run with their dogs to try to keep the tail up. They are only kidding themselves. Running will not change the temperament. Some run because the dog is not a good mover and they try to hide it with speed. Some run because they are looking ahead to Group competition where they feel they must keep up with the Afghans. Move your dog at a smooth, steady trot. If the speed demons run up your heels, let them pass.

Showing your own dog is hard. It is hard to be objective, and harder not to be nervous as you have such an emotional involvement.

Ch. Anthony of St. Hubert has the distinction of being the first Basset to win a Best in Show. Tony was totally Greenly Hall breeding, being by Ch. Duke of Greenly Hall ex Rossita of Greenly Hall, bred, owned and shown by Mark Washbond. Once he and Ch. Clown competed against each other at Morris & Essex. On that day, the judge liked a daughter of Clown, up from the classes, so neither Tony nor Clown won. Clown went Best of Opposite Sex.

Nervousness travels down the lead to the dog. Remember it is supposed to be a fun hobby. Believe us, this is hard to remember!

Don't leave immediately after your class. If you've won, you have to stay for Winners, and if you've lost, watch the rest of the breed and learn from it. One of the great losses in dog shows is the benched show, where you had to stay with your dog on display all day. By studying conversations and conformations and watching other breeds, we learned more than any book can teach.

112

Ch. Hubertus Slow Motion, owned and shown by Frank and Dorothy Hardy, won BOB at the Long Island Basset Hound Specialty.

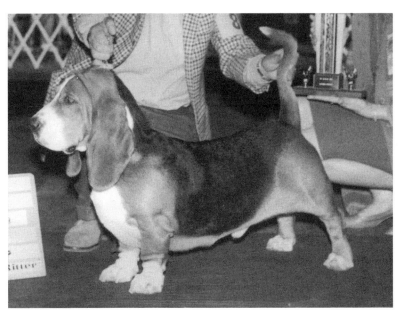

Ch. Orangepark Roy (Ch. Orangepark Eustace ex Hartshead Maybelline), owned by Mr. and Mrs. R. Wilton Meyer and shown by Jerry Rigden for owners.

Ch. Kazoo's Fredie The Freeloader was owned by J. Frank Harrison and shown by Jerry Rigden to his wins.

Don't be discouraged by early losses. The judge puts up "the dog on the day." If your dog is good and if it is shown well, your day will come.

Accept your wins and losses graciously. Do not fling ribbons down or mutter about the judge's lack of knowledge. Not only is it bad taste and poor sportsmanship, but it will get your American Kennel Club privileges lifted.

PROFESSIONAL HANDLERS

If you just can't hack showing your dog yourself—if time, nerves, family or work obligations prevent it—consider a professional handler. Watch them with their dogs, not only in the ring but at their grooming setup. Ask yourself if you want this person to take care of your dog. Ask other people in the breed about handlers. See if they are as nice to dogs when they lose as when they win. Watch their attitude in the ring. Talk with them (not when they are racing from one ring to another or otherwise busy). Find out their rates and their policy if they have a conflict between dogs. Each professional handler is an independent business person, and their procedures can differ. Ask a handler wearing a Professional Handlers Association (PHA) or Dog Handlers Guild (DHG) pin where you can get information. The handler and their rig or grooming area should be clean, neat and organized. Your dog will be in their care—would you buy a used dog from this person?

The Coldstream Pack winning Best Basset Pack at the Bryn Mawr Hound Show; Joseph J. McKenna, Master. J. J. J. McKenna, Whipper-In.

8

A Basseting We Go—
Hunting with Bassets

$\mathbf{F}$OR THE TRUE AFICIONADO of Bassets there is
only one place to be—and that is in the field enjoying the sights and
sounds as the hounds do what they were bred to do. Basseting is a
family sport and can be enjoyed by all ages, as it provides healthy
exercise in pleasant country surroundings. It is inexpensive and
involves the minimum of formality.

People involve themselves in Basseting for various reasons: to
enjoy the companionship and friendships they form in the hunting
field; for exercise—it is much more enjoyable than riding a station-
ary bicycle; to watch and listen to their favorite breed at work; and
for the thrill of tramping over the hills and through the fields and
woods.

Basseting is the art of hunting the hare or rabbit in its natural
surroundings with a pack of hounds. Basset Hounds are slower and
steadier than other breeds bred for the same purpose. They rely
entirely on the scent to follow the line and are fairly easy to follow
for this reason. Rabbit or hare hunting without the aid of a gun is a
very ancient sport, originating in France in the early 1600s.

A pack of hounds consists of five couple, minimum, but may contain as many as the Master and the aids can control. These aids are called whippers-in and are usually amateurs who have been hunting with a pack for years and understand how to control the hounds by means of voice calls, signals on a hunting horn and a whip, with which they rarely, if ever, touch the hound, the resounding *snap* of the thong being enough to startle the animal back into the pack.

Although the Huntsman and the whippers-in are in sole control of the hounds, the followers on foot, called the field, can give assistance. Those who have been members of the pack and hunt regularly with them know the names of the individual hounds and, when they stray either accidentally or on purpose, a "tally-ho" or hand signal allows the whippers-in to handle the situation.

TRADITION

Hunting season for most packs begins around the first of November and ends the first of April when weather begins to warm up. This may, however, depend upon the part of the country in which the pack is located. At the beginning of the season, it is traditional to have the hounds blessed—a very interesting ceremony and if you are a new member, this is one day that should not be missed.

The blessing of the hunt may be more legend than fact but it indeed has been handed down for many centuries and is constantly repeated in hound circles.

The religious ceremony of the "Blessing of the Hunt" on or near St. Hubert's Day, traditionally November third, is a custom that has survived since early medieval times. It has its origin in the belief that by this act, and through the intercession of St. Hubert, the hounds, riders and horses would be protected from disease or harm.

St. Hubert, the patron saint of the hunt, was born in the middle of the seventh century, a son of the Duke of Aquitaine. His early life was devoted entirely to pleasures, particularly the hunt. One Good Friday morning, when all the faithful were in church to commemorate the Passion of their Lord, Hubert, at the age of twenty-seven or twenty-eight, in defiance of pious custom, sailed forth to the chase. As he was pursuing a stag, it turned, and between its antlers was a crucifix. A voice was heard, "Unless you turn to the Lord and lead a holy life, you shall quickly go down into Hell." Hubert dismounted and, prostrating himself, said, "What wouldest Thou have me do?" The answer came, "Go seek Lambert and he will instruct you." Thus Bishop Lambert became his spiritual advisor. Hubert renounced all his honors and rank, distributed his wealth to the poor and entered the priesthood. He later became the first Bishop of Liège, and since his canonization, has been the patron saint of the hunt and the chase.

HUNTING PACKS

There are two distinct differences in packs, their ownership and the manner in which they are maintained and handled. The first is the **private pack**, in which all hounds are owned by the Master and/or Joint Master and kenneling, care, breeding and everything pertaining to the pack is the Master's responsibility. This pack is hunted usually at the discretion of the owner and may not have regular hunting days. One has to be invited to hunt with this pack and invitations may be limited to certain days and/or hours.

The second pack is considered a **subscription pack** in that one may join for a set sum and hunt at previously established times. This hunt consists of the Master and Huntsman and possibly a Joint Master, as well as a Field Secretary and a Field Master and a full hunt committee. Any subscriber to the pack may bring a guest and is responsible to the Field Secretary for payment of a capping fee to cover the guest. Most packs only allow a minimum cap of the same guest, after which said guest is requested to subscribe. Each pack may have slightly different rules pertaining to capping fee, guests or hunting times. A subscription pack issues fixture cards that list the date, time and place of the hunt. A hunt of this type usually welcomes the new and interested person, and is a wonderful way to understand the Basset and what it was bred to do. You will be asked to follow certain field customs, which are listed here:

- Always close gates behind you.
- Roll under fences or climb only at the post.
- When near stock (horses, cattle, sheep, etc.) move quietly.
- Stand still when hounds are close by.
- Don't overrun hounds at check.
- Be careful of smoking in the field. Do not litter.
- If quarry is viewed, stand where you are and point with cap or handkerchief.
- Don't shout. However, a "tally-ho" will aid the Huntsman.
- Conversation in the field should be restricted.
- Hounds must not be disturbed while hunting.
- The Field Master is appointed to add to your enjoyment of the day's sport. He is acting on direct instructions from the Huntsman. Kindly remain behind and be guided by him at all times.
- Utmost courtesy must be shown to the hunt staff.
- Visitors should always be introduced to the Master and Field Secretary.
- Anyone wishing to be excused from the field should notify the Field Master.
- Parents must be responsible for the actions and conduct of their children.
- No pets will be allowed in the hunt field.
- Never forget that we are all guests of the landowners.
- All social functions following the hunt include members and their guests.
- Dirty footgear should always be removed before entering homes after the hunt.

Now that you know the etiquette of a hunt, you should know ways to stay warm and dry on those crisp, cool fall and winter days when three or four hours following the hounds may make you question whether you wish to do this again. A warm, high-neck sweater, denim or cotton canvas trousers, wool socks and waterproof shoes

120

are the norm for the field. A warm jacket of smooth material is best, as briars and sticky-burrs are easily brushed off, and if the jacket does not have a hood, bring a head scarf or some form of warm hat—this goes for either sex. Warmth and freedom of movement are important.

Following are some hunting terms that may give you an insight into the conversation of your fellow field members. It is always good to have at least a smattering of information, and if you accompany the hunt enough times, the rest will come to you.

> **AWAY**—The quarry has "gone away" when it has left covert. Hounds are away when they have left covert on the line of the quarry.
>
> **BABBLE**—To give tongue on scent other than the hunted quarry, none at all or too faint to follow.
>
> **BLANK**—To draw blank is to fail to find any quarry.
>
> **CAST**—A planned move in search of the quarry.
>
> **CHECK**—An interruption of the run caused by hounds losing the line.
>
> **COLORS**—Collar and button colors distinguishing the uniform of one hunt from another.
>
> **COUPLE**—Two hounds; the hounds are counted in pairs.
>
> **COVERT**—A patch of woods or brush where the quarry might be found.
>
> **CRY**—The sound given by hounds when hunting.
>
> **DRAG**—Artificially laid scent.
>
> **DRAW**—Exploration of likely hiding places of quarry.
>
> **FIELD**—Those hunting.
>
> **FIELD MASTER**—The person designated by the Master (MBH) to control the field.
>
> **FIXTURE CARD**—A card listing the time and place of the meet or assembly of the hunt.
>
> **FULL CRY**—Musical chorus of hounds running their quarry with a good scent.
>
> **GROUND**—"To go to ground." To take shelter (usually underground).

HEEL—Backwards. Hounds following the line *the wrong way*.

HOLD HARD—Stand still.

HONOR—A hound "honors" by giving tongue on a line that another hound has been hunting.

HOUND—Proper term for dog or bitch in the hunting field.

HUNTSMAN—The one who controls hounds in the field.

LIFT HOUNDS—Moving hounds to a new covert.

LINE—The trail of the quarry.

MARK—The last spot where the quarry was viewed.

MARK TO GROUND—Hounds indicating quarry has gone to ground. (Technical kill)

MASTER (MASTER BASSET HOUNDS—MBH)—The person in command of the hunt in field and kennels.

MEET—The assembling of the hunt for a day's sport.

OPEN—A hound is said to open when first giving tongue on a line.

PACK—Generic term for the working units of hounds.

QUARRY—An animal being hunted.

RIOT—Anything hounds might hunt that they should not.

SCENT—Smell left by quarry.

SPEAK—To give tongue (cry) and give voice when on the line.

STERN—Tail of the hound.

TALLY-HO—The call made when quarry is viewed.

TAIL HOUNDS—Hounds that are running some distance behind the pack.

VIEW—See the quarry.

WHIPPER-IN—A staff member who assists the Huntsman.

WORRY—Hounds fighting over quarry that has been killed.

HAPPY HUNTING!

9

Veterinary Aspects and Breeding of the Basset Hound

by Calvin Moon, VMD

IT HAS BEEN my pleasure to be associated with two large Basset kennels in New Jersey for the past forty years. This experience has impressed me with the inherent soundness of the Basset Hound. While this hound is one of the chondrodystrophoid breeds when compared to some of the other popular pure-bred dogs, there appear to be relatively few heriditary defects associated with the Basset Hound.

BREEDING

If owners decide to breed their bitch, they should rely upon the knowledge and services of a reputable breeder. One of the most frequent mistakes the novice breeder makes is to secure the male and bitch in an enclosure and let nature take its course. Such a mating would approach an immaculate conception in the case of the

Basset. The male usually requires assistance in guiding the penis into the bitch's vagina. Naturally this requires control of both the dog and the bitch with collar and leash.

Timing of ovulation is an important consideration. Acceptance of the male is signified by the bitch flagging her tail and her willingness to accept attempts at mounting by the male. This generally occurs on the tenth day following the first notice of bleeding. Often ovulation timing can be frustrating and veterinary assistance may be needed. This can be fairly accurately predicted on the basis of vaginal cytology, by way of smears, or by measurement of blood progesterone levels.

WHELPING

Normal gestation takes fifty-seven to sixty-seven days, with the average being sixty-two or sixty-three days. A clear discharge is usually noted from the vagina. The body temperature will drop below 100 degrees F. Whelping will usually occur within twenty-four hours. This process is mraked by hard abdominal contractions.

A pup should be presented within three hours. Any interval longer than this may denote serious trouble and will require veterinary intervention. Whelping may be a long session in the Basset Hound, and a Caesarean section is often required. Radiographs may be needed to determine if the bitch is finished whelping. She should be examined by a veterinarian within twenty-four hours after whelping to check for any puppies or retained placenta, and to be sure that the uterus is returning to normal (involution). Also, an injection of pituitary oxytocin may be required to aid involution and let down milk. The puppies may also be checked at this time for any birth defects such as cleft palate, swimmers, defective limbs or umbilical defects.

MEDICAL PROBLEMS

A mention of **pyometra** is appropriate in discussing breeding and medical aspects of the bitch. Often an uninformed owner may present a bitch for breeding, thinking that the bloody discharge present is a sign of estrus. *In reality, this may be the first sign of an open pyometra.* If this is a valuable breeding bitch, the judicious use of prostaglandins may get her back to sound breeding condition and for an important brood bitch is preferable to spaying. *A closed pyometra* may be more difficult to suspect, but is generally seen in an older bitch that may never have had a litter or may have had one at an earlier age.

Signs of a closed pyometra usually include increased water consumption and increased frequency of urination. There is generally sluggishness and a poor appetite. Your veterinarian can make a diagnosis based on radiographs and a Complete Blood Count. This condition may require an ovario-hysterectomy (spaying) to save the bitch's life, since she may be critically ill.

Perhaps the most common presentation to the vet is for **dermatitis**. The single most prevalent condition is for *flea allergy dermatitis*. This is manifested by a thin hair coat over the caudal-lumbar (back) area (near the tail) with redness and a severe persistent pruritus sometimes called hot spots. There are numerous flea control products on the market but all require periodic treatments and also eradication of fleas in the kennel or home.

Seborrhea is a familial disease sometimes found in Basset Hounds. It is marked by a scaly, greasy coat with tightly adherent scaly patches on the back and chest. There are remedies available that include tar-sulfur shampoos and anti-bacterial shampoos such as Oxydex. Treatment generally is necessary throughout the life of the dog.

While the Basset Hound has no predisposition for hypothyroidism, this can cause seborrhea. Treatment with thyroid replacement drugs such as synthroid may correct the seborrhea.

Inversion of the eyelids (**entropion**) or excessive drooping of the lower lids (**ectropion**) does occur in the Basset Hound breed. Generally this condition requires surgical intervention for correction.

Lip-fold dermatitis can be a problem. This is an infection present in the crease in the lower lip. Treatment consists of routine cleansing with a bacteriocidal soap and topical application of anti-bacterial ointment.

Routine ear care is a necessity in the breed because of the large pendulous ear, which predisposes the breed to **ear infection**. This entails at least weekly irrigation with a product that both dissolves wax and disinfects the ear. Such products are readily obtainable. More serious conditions should be diagnosed by the veterinarian using bacterial and fungal ear cultures and then prescribing appropriate medications. Surgical intervention is often needed in chronic cases.

Anal sac impaction or infection is not unusual, especially in a household pet that gets little exercise. Manual expression of the gland by inserting a finger in the anus and applying pressure to squeeze the gland will correct most problems. Infections will require insertion of antibiotic ointment into the sac and should be repeated two or three times by your vet. Surgical removal of the anal sacs may be necessary in some chronic cases.

The rather large paws of the Basset Hound predisposes the breed to **interdigital infections** involving the web between the digits. Some are caused by grass allergies, contact dermatitis from products used to clean runs or from foreign bodies such as grass awns or gravel penetrating the web. Proper diagnosis will enable you to eliminate the cause.

The Basset does have a predilection for **sebaceous gland tumors** in the skin. These are usually small, round lumps in the skin and contain a greasy, whitish material. Such cysts may remain small for some time, but can enlarge or ulcerate and become infected. In such cases surgical intervention is necessary.

INFECTIOUS DISEASES

Routine immunizations have practically eliminated canine **distemper, hepatitis** and **leptospirosis** as major problems in a kennel or for the individual pet owner.

Parvovirus remains a serious threat in spite of vaccination. Veterinarians have found that giving a final parvo vaccine at four months of age is necessary to confer immunity. Breeds such as the Doberman Pinscher, the Rottweiler and the German Shepherd Dog seem to be especially susceptible to parvo. Early in the history of this disease recovery often left the pup with serious heart disease. More recently this has not been observed so frequently.

A newly recognized problem is Borreliosis or **Lyme disease**. Except for the acute case, presented with high fever and joint swelling, the diagnosis can be a problem. Diagnosis is based on the measurement of IgG and IgM antibodies in the blood. Treatment with specific antibiotics for three to four weeks generally is effective. A new vaccine is available that has proven to be effective in field tests. Since Lyme disease is carried primarily by the deer tick, it would be prudent for the kennel or individual dog owner to practice good tick control and vaccination if they are located in an area with a large deer population. This would apply especially to those owners who enter their dogs in Field Trials.

Canine infectious brucellosis is another disease that may threaten a breeding kennel. Another name for this disease is infectious abortion and it results in aborted fetuses and infertility. The infection can be spread by breeding. This disease can occur in the Basset Hound as well as virtually every breed. A Basset dog or bitch used for breeding should be tested negative for the disease. This blood test is readily performed by your vet. Since there is no permanent cure for this disease, infected animals should not be used for breeding since they may spread the disease through contact with semen, urine, vaginal discharges, fetal membranes or milk; affected dogs should be euthanized.

ORTHOPEDIC PROBLEMS

As one of the chondrodystrophic breeds, the Basset Hound does present some **achondroplastic changes** in the bones. For instance, the short legs in relation to body size are apparently controlled by an unknown number of genes. The short legs are incompletely dominant to long legs since selective breeding can produce long legs within six generations.

Humeral-ulnar subluxation (dislocation of these two bones at the elbow) has been reported in the breed. This elbow problem

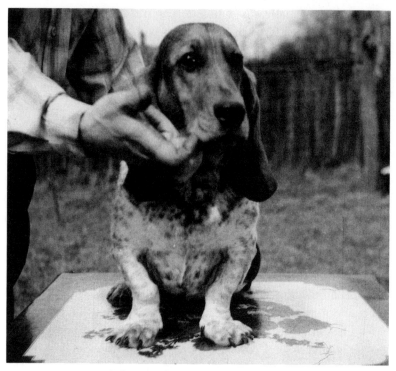

A Basset with orthopedic problems.

can only be corrected surgically. Without such correction, arthritic changes are heightened and lameness can present itself.

Cervical vertebral instability of C2-3 or C3-4 has been reported in the breed. Dogs can be affected at any age, but most cases are under eight months of age. These pups are generally unable to walk normally, hence the term "wobbler."

Foreleg lameness caused by bowing of the radius can happen as a result of injury to the distal growth plate of the ulna. This will allow the radius (the larger bone in the foreleg) to grow while the ulna stops growing or grows at a slower rate, resulting in bending of the radius.

Osteochondritis Dessicans of the shoulder is the result of trauma to the articular cartilage, causing severe lameness. Loose pieces of detached cartilage or flaps of cartilage interfere with

A Basset with an improper front, weak pasterns and very long nails which can combine to bring on severe movement problems.

smooth joint motion. **OCD** occurs in dogs from six months to two years of age. The condition can heal with prolonged rest or may require surgical repair.

Hypertrophic osteodystrophy usually occurs in dogs under a year of age and results in fever, swelling of the distal radius and ulna and lameness. The disease will generally run its course and is controlled with pain relievers such as aspirin. Some individuals have been so severely affected that they must be euthanized.

Panosteitis is an inflammation of the long bones in dogs from six months to two years of age. It can occur in the *humerus, radius, femur and tibia*. Diagnosis is made from radiographs of the affected bones. Treatment consists of anti-inflammatory drugs such as aspirin or its analogues. The condition can recur in different bones.

Stifle (knee) injuries are fairly common. The knee joint is stabilized by the cranial and posterior cruciate ligaments within the joint and the lateral and medial collateral ligaments outside of the joint. Most commonly the cranial cruciate ligament ruptures, creating a very unstable joint and severe lameness. The knee may heal enough to allow weight bearing after about three months provided the dog is given complete rest. Even so the instability of the joint will lead to severe arthritic changes in the knee. Surgical repair of the injury results in a much more stable joint and a more rapid return to normal.

Luxation of the patella (kneecap) is an affliction of the hind legs. Normally the kneecap slides in a groove at the end of the femur as the knee is flexed. A ridge on each side of this groove keeps it in place. If the groove is too shallow, or the ridges too low, the kneecap will slip to one side or the other, thus luxating and causing lameness. The defect generally is apparent after the age of six months. This defect is a recessive polygenic and multi-focal inheritance. Breeders should select against it by not breeding parents or littermates of affected dogs. The defect can be repaired surgically.

Elbow dysplasia results when the anconeal process of the ulna fails to ossify, that is, become normal bone. This produces a piece of loose bone in the elbow joint that must be removed surgically to cure the lameness. This defect can be recognized by severe lameness and pain and swelling of the elbow joint. Diagnosis is made by X-ray of the affected elbow.

SOME INHERITED DEFECTS IN THE BREED

An **X-linked** severe **immunodeficiency** caused by an abnormal gene located on the X chromosome, has been reported in the Basset Hound. This results in bacterial and viral infections that may lead to the death of affected pups. Normal growth is retarded, producing stunted, unhealthy pups. Defects in the immune system may be caused by undetectable IgA, low IgG or normal IgM, if these antibodies do not exist in the correct structure or amount to fight infection.

Cryptorchidism has been noted in some lines within the breed. This is the retention of one testicle within the abdominal cavity. This is a sex-linked recessive genetic expression carried by the bitch, but both sire and dam must carry the trait for it to occur. Surgical correction of this condition is discouraged by the American Kennel Club and disqualifies such animals from being shown.

Basset Hounds are above average risk for the occurrence of **inguinal hernia**. This is a bulging of abdominal organs or fat through the inguinal canal (groin). Such hernias can become strangulated, shutting off the blood supply to those organs, resulting in a hard, painful swelling that can be life-threatening by causing peritonitis. Such a condition would require immediate surgery. These hernias should be corrected surgically before they strangulate. The condition is thought to be hereditary and such individuals should not be used for breeding.

A **familial platelet disorder** has been reported in the Basset Hound. This is an autosomal trait that is dominant or dominant with incomplete expression. Both sexes can be affected. Platelets are part of the blood necessary for clotting. While there are ample numbers present, they have decreased stickiness. The result of this defect is severe bleeding from injuries or surgery. Only heroic measures, such as a blood transfusion, may save the affected dog. The breeding that produces such animals should not be repeated.

Myoclonus epilepsy or Laforas disease was reported in the Basset in Holland in 1970. This is a storage defect of neuronal glycoprotein in the nervous system. The clinical signs are somnolence, incoordination, convulsions and progressive deterioration.

Von Willebrand's disease is another derangement of the clotting mechanism of the blood. The Basset has a prevalence of 15 percent or greater. Since the Basset is at relatively low risk, severe hemorrhage during injury of a mild nature or during routine surgery may be the only clue to the presence of the problem. A blood transfusion is sometimes needed to control hemorrhage.

Bassets may be troubled with either **primary or secondary glaucoma**. Symptoms are a bulging painful eye caused by increased intra-ocular pressure. This is sometimes associated with luxation of the lens. Mesodermal dysgenesis leading to glaucoma has been reported.

Conjunctivitis is an inflammation of the third eyelid or the tissues lining the lids. Being a field dog, the Basset is liable to collect dust, weed awns or pollen in these tissues, causing irritation and tearing. Flushing of the eye with a proprietary eye wash may alleviate the problem, but generally veterinary care is needed.

Cataracts, or opacities of the lens, are commonly seen. A blue, white or gray color is seen in the eye and usually results in some loss of vision. A bluish color in the lens of the older animal is called nuclear sclerosis and is not a cataract. This too can cause visual deficiencies. The sudden onset of cataracts may be caused by the presence of diabetes. Your vet will always check the animal's blood sugar level to determine if diabetes is present. Cataracts can be corrected by surgical removal of the lens and will restore some vision in many cases.

Eye injuries such as briar scratches to the cornea (the clear part of the eye) can result in infection and ulceration. Very small scratches to the cornea may only be seen by the use of a fluorescein stain applied by the vet. Eye injuries should be treated quickly by the vet since neglect can cause loss of vision or even necessitate removal of the eye.

URINARY TRACT DISORDERS

Stone formation either in the **kidney or urinary bladder** is not uncommon in the Basset. Cysteine calculi have frequently been reported in the breed. These stones result from an inherited defect in the proximal tubules of the kidney, which allows excessive urinary excretion of cystine, an amino acid. Since cystine is insoluble in urine, precipitation and formation of calculi (stones) is the result. The stones are generally removed surgically and prescription diets may prevent recurrence. These stones occur predominantly in male dogs and recurrence is usual.

Infections of the **urinary tract** can occur in any breed. The initial signs are drinking excess water and frequent urination. Veterinarians generally can identify the bacterial pathogen by culture and antibiotic sensitivity testing of the urine. A two- or three-week course of the appropriate antibiotic will resolve the problem.

GASTROINTESTINAL TRACT

Because of the Basset Hound's conformation (deep chest) **bloat** (dilatation and torsion of the stomach) can occur. While this condition is more common in giant and large breed dogs, it has been reported in the Basset. *Prompt recognition of the problem is crucial.* Marked distension of the abdomen, unproductive attempts to vomit and obvious pain and distress are the initial symptoms. Prompt intubation of the stomach will relieve the gas and is usually performed by a veterinarian. Treatment for shock is necessary and *surgical intervention is required to correct a torsion.* Part of the surgical repair consists of tying down the stomach to the abdominal wall. There are several methods to accomplish this and the surgeon will generally do what has proven to be most effective based on his or her experience.

Torsion of the spleen has also occurred in the Basset and can happen in conjunction with torsion of the stomach or can occur independently. Here again prompt surgical intervention will save the animal. In most cases the spleen will have to be removed during this process.

CONCLUSION

In closing this chapter it is important to note that while some genetic problems are present in the breed, they are not a major problem. In the bibliography of *Genetics for Dog Breeders*, by

Frederick B. Hutt of Cornell University, listing approximately 250 references, there are none relating to the Basset Hound. Certainly this indicates that the breed is inherently healthy and will provide owners with many carefree years of companionship.

Veterinary Bibliography

Barnett, K. C. "Primary Glaucoma in Dogs." *JAVMA* 145 (1962): 1081–1091.

Case, L. C., et al. "Cystine-Containing Urinary Calculi in Dogs: 102 Cases (1981–1989)." *JAVMA* 201, no. 1 (1992): 129–133.

The Compendium, 14, no. 7. Hoskins, Johnny D., "Congenital Defects of the Dog," "Cervical Vertebral Instability," table p. 873, (1992).

Dodds, W. J. "Inherited Hemorrhagic Disorders." *JAAHA* 11 (1975): 366–373.

Erickson, F., et al. "Congenital Defects in Dogs: A Special Reference For Practitioners." Ralston-Purina reprint from *Canine Practice*. Santa Barbara: Veterinary Practice Publ., 1978.

Hutt, Frederick B. Chap. 12 in *Genetics for Dog Breeders*. San Francisco: W. H. Freeman and Co., 1979.

Johnson, I. B., and F. Lotz. "Familial Platelet Disorder." *Can Vet J* 20 (1979): 211–215.

Jones and Hunt, *Veterinary Pathology*, 5 ed. Philadelphia: 1983. "Laforas Disease (Myoclonus Epilepsy), Holland, 1970."

Kirk, R. W., and S. I. Bistner. "Hereditary Defects in Dogs," table 124. In *Handbook of Veterinary Procedures and Emergency Treatment*. Philadelphia: W. B. Saunders Co., 1975.

Lau, R. E. "Inherited Premature Closure of the Distal Ulnar Physis." *JAAHA* 13 (1977): 609–612.

Martin, C. L., and M. Wyman. "Glaucoma in the Basset Hound." *JAVMA* 153 (1968): 1320–1327.

Patterson, D. F., et al. ACVIM Proceedings Sixth Annual Veterinary Medical Forum, 1988.

10

The Basset Hound in Canada

by R. C. and P. M. Waterhouse

THE ARRIVAL of the Basset Hound in Canada is somewhat obscured in the mists of time. However, it is generally known that three Basset Hounds were entered in a show held in 1936; this was the year the Canadian Kennel Club recognized the breed.

Recorded in the early Stud Books were nine individual registrations. In order for this to transpire and receive recognition by the Canadian Kennel Club, there had to be some established breeders to develope definite bloodlines.

Information regarding the breeders in those earlier times is almost nonexistent; however, Dorothy Grant of Port Hope, Ontario, can be given recognition as the first breeder in Canada. In 1943, Dorothy Grant purchased Maytime Peg O' My Heart, bred by Claude M. Smith of Grand Rapids, Michigan. Her other early owners were Mrs. Harold Fogelson and Dorothy Grant a second time. The sire of this bitch was Ch. Promise of Greenly Hall (A434465) ex Nottke's

Canadian and American Ch. Bow-Ridge's Lena Horne was Best of Breed at the Basset Hound Club of Canada Specialty under breeder/judge Michael Sosne. Bow-Ridge Kennels is owned by Lou and Roxanna Bowman.

Pat (by Kilsyth Artist ex Staridge Pallas). With this hound Miss Grant acquitted herself extremely well in the United States at such shows as Westminster and Westchester.

Again, it is unfortunate to relate that without the aid of recorded facts of the 1940s and 1950s few positive facts can be uncovered. It appears that some of the breeders who were active during this time in Eastern Canada were the Hendersons, and the Purdys of Ontario, as well as the Hunts from Ottawa. In central Canada the Stinsons of Manitoba were becoming recognized, and Rosemary Osselton and Ron Sless were gaining recognition in the West on Vancouver Island.

In 1959, a hound that would later be known as Am. Can. Ch. Whistledown Commando was whelped in Michigan. Commando was to become the first Basset Hound to win an all-breed Best in Show award in Canada. This hound played a very significant role in Canadian Basset history. He is to be found in the pedigrees of such well-known kennels as Westacre (Carter), Sand-Dell (Sandell) and Bow-Ridge (Bowman).

136

THE BASSET HOUND CLUB OF CANADA

On January 30, 1960, the Basset Hound Club of Canada was formed in Ontario. The prime interests of its original members were breeding and showing in Conformation, although interest and awareness of Obedience and working in the field with their hounds began to blossom.

In September of 1961 the Club members organized their first Specialty show; the exact date was the twenty-third. Best of Breed went to a hound owned by Dorothy Hurry, Am. Ch. Ike of Blue Hill; he repeated this win in 1962, and again in 1964 to retire the trophy. It was not until October 31, 1982, that the first club-sponsored Field Trial was held at the Wentworth Beagle Club under licensed Beagle judges.

OTHER CLUBS

More interest in the breed was developing in the early 1960s out west in British Columbia, resulting in a group of fanciers getting together and forming a club that they logically named the Basset Hound Club of British Columbia. It was not until later in that decade that this club put on the first of many successful Specialties held over the years. Working in the field was also achieved, but in an unofficial capacity. The club is still active with Basset Hound Rescue, which is an onerous and sensitive issue; from the onset this work has been in the capable hands of Mr. Crawford Bell, to which the people involved in Bassets in the British Columbia area are greatly indebted.

On a lighter note, a tradition begun and sponsored by the BHC of British Columbia is the popular and much publicized Annual Basset Walk, which is held during spring, rain or shine, in Vancouver's beautiful Stanley Park. Hundreds of spectators turn out for this event, having done so for almost three decades. Everyone is welcome to participate with or without a hound, and there is a general air of camaraderie felt throughout.

As the popularity of the Basset hound flourished across Canada, other small groups got together and formed various organizations, striving toward the betterment of the breed, and the general welfare and protection of the Basset Hound.

CANADIAN-BRED BASSET HOUNDS

The Early Days

Listed below are the first entries of Basset Hounds in the CKC Stud Book. There is no record of Charles Perrault breeding—Dorothy Grant can be given recognition as the first breeder in Canada.

> **BESS OF BANBURY** (179031) A677726, Female, white & tan, blue-ticked, born October 7, 1942, bred by Consuelo U. Ford, Old Chatam, NY, U.S.A.; 2nd owner, Charles Perrault, Montreal, Que.; *Sire*—Bijou Moonstone of Banbury 2nd A429691 (Kilsyth Banker [Kilsyth Bunker—Kilsyth Fury]) Edwina ([Ch. Reddy 2nd—Walhampton Nicety]) *Dam*—Bijou Matrix of Banbury A575464 (Bijou Moonstone of Banbury 2nd [Kilsyth Banker—Edwina]) Bijou Pearl of Banbury ([Chasseur—Edwina]).

> **MAYTIME PEG O' MY HEART** (183005) A709265, Female, black, white & tan, born May 5, 1943, bred by Claude R. Smith, Grand Rapids, MI, U.S.A.; 2nd owner, Mrs. Harold Fogleson, East Lansing, MI, U.S.A.; 3rd owner, Dorothy Grant, Port Hope, Ont.; *Sire*—Ch. Promise of Greenly Hall A434465 (Nottke's Pat [Kilsyth Artist—Staridge Pallas) Ch. Peg O' My Heart ([Ch. Smith's Red Powder—Nottke's Venus]). *Dam*—Melancholy Baby A646978 (Ch. Duke of Greenly Hall [Venus's Black Mischief—White's Jaconde] Kiernan's Mitz [Chasseur—Edwina]).

SPOT OF BANBURY (179032) + 677727, Male, white, tan & black, born June 5, 1942, bred by Consuelo U. Ford, Old Chatam, NY, U.S.A.; 2nd owner, Charles Perrault, Montreal, Que.; *Sire*—Ch. Bijou Rhinestone of Banbury A306409 (Chasseur [Maple Drive Maxim—Maple Drive Topsey] Edwina [Ch. Reddy 2nd—Walhampton Nicety]). *Dam*—Bijou Sapphire of Banbury A275841 (Chasseur [Maple Drive Maxim—Maple Drive Topsey] Stanco Lady [Amir of Reynalton—Stanco Koto]).

BASSET HOUND LINES IN CANADA

Chantinghall

A respected name in Basset Hounds since 1959 is that of Jim and Rosemary McKnight, who came to Canada from England where they were registered with the Kennel Club. In England they had

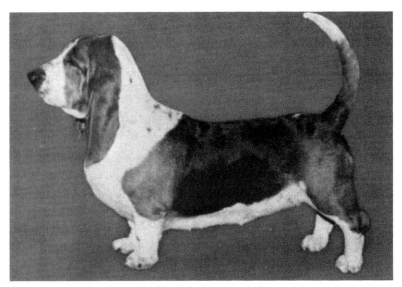

Canadian and American Ch. Chantinghall Airs 'n Graces. A top winning bitch in Canadian Basset history; bred and owned by Rosemary McKnight.

considerable success in the whelping box and in the show ring. Chantinghall is in the pedigrees of many notable English kennels. Upon coming to Wainfleet, Ontario, in 1967 with some of their stock, they registered their prefix with the Canadian Kennel Club, thus the same prefix is registered in two countries.

One of their first attempts to integrate the English and American Basset Hound was to purchase Can. & Am. Ch. Solitude Creek Sophocles from the United States. This dog became a strong influence on the breed in Canada. The McKnights continued breeding and showing successfully over the years. It can be noted that many of the Kennels in Canada have Chantinghall stock as their foundation Bassets. Others have found the Chantinghall line fit in very well with what they already have, thus making it possible to further strengthen their own lines.

Jim and Rosemary McKnight promoted their stock from various litters. One well-known Basset was Can. & Am. Ch. Chantinghall Airs in Graces, a beautiful bitch who acquitted herself very well in the show ring.

At this time the McKnights have retired from active breeding and showing, but still maintain a keen interest in the breed. Rosemary McKnight continues her role as a well-respected all-breed judge, being very much in demand. The Chantinghall era will remain alive in the backgrounds of Basset Hounds yet to come.

Westacres

At the beginning of another decade, 1960, Mr. and Mrs. Fred Carter of Oakville, Ontario, had lost their Cocker Spaniel. Although feeling very depressed, they decided they would like to acquire another dog. While reading the pet column of the local newspaper, they came across an advertisement that led them to Ron and Joey Purdy, where they saw and immediately fell in love with a Basset puppy whom they named Schauffleins Logy. This boy introduced the Carters to the world of Basset Hounds and dog shows.

Eventually they acquired a bitch, Hartshead Fanfare, from Effie and Emil Seitz. This bitch became the foundation bitch for Westacres Kennel, and was eventually mated to Logy. From different litters she produced Ch. Westacres Queen Valli and Ch. West-acres Little Nell, to name two of the many that went on to gain their championships. Valli was subsequently mated to her grandfather, Ch. Whistledown Commando, producing the very well-known hound Ch. Westacres Hugo the Red, who covered himself with untold glory. At the first show of shows sponsored by Ralston-Purina, Hugo came away with the ultimate Best in Show ribbon. Westacres Basset Hounds have undoubtedly made a significant contribution to various breeding programs.

Mr. Carter had become very much involved in the Society for Prevention of Cruelty to Animals, and, of course, he was also active as a dog show judge. It was a great shock to the dog fancy to learn of his untimely death.

Scotts-Moore

Scotts-Moore, registered, started in Basset Hounds in 1972 with the purchase of Ch. Bow-Ridge's Honeybun.

In 1973, Ch. Sand-Dell's Sandy Girl was purchased from Ron Sandell. Sandy produced thirteen champions for the Scotts-Moore Kennel, including an international champion with a CD title and a Danish Champion. Sandy had offspring in four countries.

In recent years those at Scotts-Moore owned and co-owned many champions and Obedience dogs with Bone-A-Part Basset Hounds in Florida, and have also successfully shown and bred those dogs since 1983, when State of the Art, "Artie," arrived at Scotts-Moore.

Scotts-Moore own and co-own three Best in Show hounds, and the same hounds are Specialty winners in Canada and in the United States. There are Scotts-Moore Basset Hounds on three continents and five countries.

Sand-Dell's

Located in Eastern Canada, the kennel that has made a definite impact on the breed as a whole in Canada is Sand-Dell's. Established June 17, 1965, with the importation of a young female from Nancy Evans Kennel in Arizona, who was named Jocamine's Cherry Jubilee, whelped February 21, 1964, by Am. Ch. Santana-Mandeville J. P. Morgan ex Jocamine's Diana. Thus it all began for Sand-Dell's. Cherry obtained her Canadian title in short order and then moved on to produce some very fine Basset Hounds. Her first litter was sired by Am. Ch. Nancy Evans Billy the Kid, who eventually became the sire of fifty champions.

From the above litter Mr. Sandell kept three of the best females as his foundation stock.

In 1968, Mr. Sandell purchased Can. Ch. Whistledown Commando from Mrs. R. Purdy. This male was bred to several of the Sand-Dell females with excellent results. One breeding was to a Cherry daughter, called Sand-Dell's Dark Eyed Nancy, who in turn produced Ch. Sand-Dell's Century Boy, Sand-Dell's Century Girl and Sand-Dell's Dixie Belle. Most of the present-day Sand-Dell breeding stems from these hounds. Jim and Rosemary McKnight, who at that time owned Can. & Am. Ch. Solitude Creek Sophocles, top Basset in Canada in 1972, visited the Sandells in 1974. Sophocles was descended from the Lyn Mar Acres bloodlines, and so it

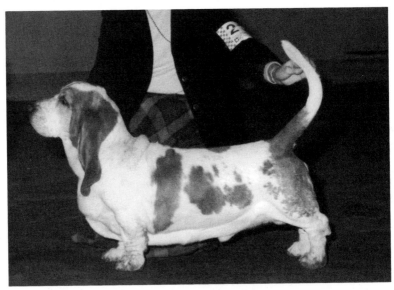

Canadian, American and Bermudan Ch. Scotts-Moore Seymour, CD

142

Ch. Sand-Dell's Anastasia, was Best of Winners at the 1973 Basset Hound Club of America National, shown by her owner.

was a unanimous decision to combine the Sand-Dell lines with those of Sophocles, which resulted in the continued success of this kennel in both the whelping box and show ring.

Mr. Sandell has an ongoing love affair with Basset Hounds. There are fifty-two champions recorded at Sand-Dell's. Some of the hounds that have made an impact on the breed are listed below:

Ch. Jocamine's Cherry Jubilee
Ch. Sand-Dell's Black Raspution
Ch. Sand-Dell's Anastasia
Ch. Sand-Dell's Sandy Girl (dam of eleven champions)
Ch. Sand-Dell's Sibin O'Kendorba
Ch. Longbay's Black Diamond
    San-Dell's Snoopy Girl

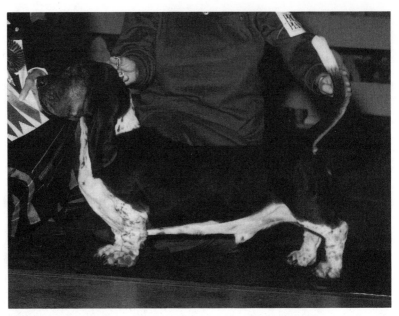

Ch. Longbays Nightcap, Winners Dog at the Basset Hound Club of America National, 1988. Longbay Kennels are owned by John and Carmen Huggins, Ontario, Canada.

Heathrow–Pyperwynd

In the early 1960s, Dick and Pat Waterhouse of Vancouver, British Columbia, started to fly the Basset flag. Their first Basset was just a pet, but they became so enchanted with the breed that they decided to find another female as a companion for the one they already had. In their quest, they spotted an advertisement in the newspaper for a female Basset puppy, which was, on inquiry, a show prospect. At that time showing dogs was not on the agenda. However, on taking the puppy home, they decided to work with the breeder and take the puppy to some matches. Needless to say, that was the beginnings of showing for all the family.

Meeting with a very small measure of success in the show ring and less in the whelping box, a decision was made to purchase new stock. Importing hounds from the well-known Forest Bay Kennel brought some merit; however experience is a good teacher and lessons had been learned.

144

About this time Fate took a hand and presented Dick and Pat with the opportunity to purchase a young red and white male puppy named Bevlees Injun Joe. Joe turned out to be a super show dog who loved every minute of the show business. He and Jim Campbell made a name for themselves in record time. Joe also finished his American championship under the expert handling of the now-deceased Marvin Cates. Joe's descendants have inherited his love of the show ring.

At this time it was decided that what was needed was a linebred quality bitch, if one could be found. Eventually Margaret Walton sent a tri-colored five-month-old bitch, Lyn Mar Acres Tosca. She had a gorgeous head and arch of neck, absolutely sound front and rear, and even as a puppy, moved like a well-oiled machine. Thus began a success story far beyond their expectations. This success was achieved with very few litters over those early years. Because of a very busy working life-style, the whelping box only came out occasionally, so the breedings had to be well chosen. Lyn Mar Acres Tosca was lost to cancer at a relatively early age, but she left those at Heathrow and Pyperwynd a tremendous legacy to continue breeding and showing.

The name "Heathrow" gradually started to cover itself with glory. American and Canadian Specialty winners came from the first Tosca litter. From the second litter came their first Best in Show bitch, Am. & Can. Ch. Heathrow's Classic Image. One of Heathrow's most treasured wins came with Can. & Am. Ch. Heathrow's Touch of Minx—Best in Specialty under noted breeder/judge Giuseppe Benelli.

In 1983 their daughter, Susan, and her husband, Harold Pybus, who already bred and showed Irish Setters, decided to breed Basset Hounds under the "Pyperwynd" prefix, planning, of course, to work within the Heathrow bloodlines. They also started out with their own bitch, Jubilations First Class, out of Ch. Heathrow's Class 'n Brass ex Chantinghalls Honey Chile. This bitch was taken to Can. & Am. Ch. Heathrow's A Touch of Class, resulting in the litter that produced Can. & Am. Ber. Ch. Pyperwynds I'm Reddie Freddie.

Hard work and sorrow does pay off and tend to fade into

A family portrait of three generations of top winners: Canadian, American and Bermudan Ch. Pyperwynd I'm Reddie Freddie, owned by Harold and Susan Pybus. Freddie is the sire of Canadian and American Ch. Heathrow's Carry On Class Act owned by John A. Hackley, Tacoma, WA, and was handled by Judy Webb to his great wins. Freddie's grandson is Canadian and American Ch. Sir Ethan's Basil of Heathrow owned by Heathrow and Pyperwynd. All three generations are Best in Show and Specialty winners.

the mists of time when you consider the successful hounds whose individual accomplishments are as follows:

     Can. & Am. Ch. Heathrow's
     A Touch of Class...............................Sire of Freddie
     Can. & Am. Ch. Heathrow's
     Classic Image ....Multiple BIS
                                             &
                                          Multiple Specialty
                                          BOS BHCA 1983
     Can. & Am. Ber. Ch. Pyperwynd
     I'm Reddie Freddie............................Sire of Mike
     Can. & Am. Ch. Heathrow's
     Carry on Class Act ....Sire of Basil
     Can. & Am. Ch. Sir Ethans
     Basil of Heathrow

Freddie, Mike and Basil are all multiple Best in Show winners and Specialty show winners. During his show career Freddie garnered

146

Canadian and American Ch. Sir Ethan's Basil of Heathrow, a top winner in both Canada and the United States. Sired by Ch. Heathrow's Carry On Class Act ex Heathrow's Nothing But Klass, Basil was bred by Michael and Tara Dyde and owned by R. C. and P. M. Waterhouse and H. J. Pybus. Basil was Best of Breed at the Basset Hound Club of America National—1992.

(Animal World Studio)

many trophies and ribbons. He was shown a total of 219 times in Canada with the following results:

210 Best of Breeds
136 Group Firsts
57 Other Group Placings
34 all-breed Best in Shows
10 Specialty Best of Breeds

In 1988, Freddie was number one Basset Hound, number one Hound overall and number three all-breeds. In 1989 he was number one Basset hound, number two Hound and number nine All-Breeds.

While Freddie was making a track record in Canada, his son, Mike, owned by John A. Hackley, Tacoma, Washington, was endeavoring to excel in the United States. Am. & Can. Ch. Heathrow's Carry On Class Act became number one Basset Hound in the U.S. in 1989. It is believed that this was the first time that a father and son combination were number one at the same time.

Heathrow and their class act are carrying on.

Contributions to the Basset Hound Breed

We would like to mention some of the breeders who have made past contributions to this wonderful breed, and also some newer fanciers to this sport, who will endeavor to continue breeding and caring for the Basset Hound in true Canadian tradition.

Quebec	R. & I. Muncey	(Idaron)
	Martine Ouimet	(Delorblanc)
Ontario	Rob & Jan Albon	(Verulam)
	Burt & Rosa Dancocks	(Wilburdan)
	J. & S. McMillan	(Ballyhowl)
	J. & P. Merritt	(Danhewly)
	E. & I. Sadler	(Clayhanger)
Manitoba	Glenoria Molnar	(Blackjack)
	W. & B. Seepish	(Lone Star)
Saskatchewan	Linda Kraft	(Raintree)

Alberta..............	J. & L. Bruton	(Brujean)
	Debbie Fleece	(Blaz'n Saddle)
	F. & C. Thornton	(Blackstar)
	B. & L. Trypka	(Barn Bay)
British Columbia...	P. & B. Belanger	(Belforrest)
	Cheryl Coughlan	(Hardtimes)
	Alan & Susan Goad	(Sualla)
	Patricia Nuttall	(Jubalation)
	Lorna Rindal	(Torcroft)
	Jean Rondpre	(Keenleyside)
	A. & J. Soderquist	(Arjan)
	Bonnie Tetlock	(Bonerlea)

Foyewyn Flirtie of Maycombe By Ch. Wingjays Ptolemy ex Foyewyn Berenice; breeder Mrs. S. A. Goodwin. Owned and shown by Mildred Seiffert to two CCs and Best of Breed at the Club show. Imported by Lyn Mar Acres.

150

11

The Basset Hound Around the World

ENGLAND

Much has already been covered regarding the Basset Hound in England, its beginning, the early Standards and imports-exports.

The Basset Hound Club was founded in 1884 and for a number of years went along very well but in 1921 it was dissolved. The primary reason being the differences of opinion between the hunting people and the show (bench) people. The breed carried on without a club, and after the end of World War II was in a very poor way. Had it not been for the efforts of Peggy Keevil and her Grims Hounds, many believe that Bassets might well have been extinct as a pure breed in England. Not only did she keep her best hounds going, but also imported three dog hounds from France, the best known of these being Ulema de Barly.

Angela Hodson purchased her first hound from Grims and, when she asked about a club, was told that many had asked this same question but sufficient support did not seem to be there to

The Grim's Basset Hound Pack, later to be known as The Albany Bassets, the official pack of the Basset Hound Club, John Evans, MBH.

support one. The Kennel Club at that time required twenty-five people to subscribe two guineas each in order to form a new club.

After buying puppies from Mrs. Hodson's first litter, several of the new owners also inquired about joining a club. At long last, Miss Keevil and Mrs. Hodson got together and wrote to all they thought might be interested, the result being a newly formed Basset Hound Club in 1954. The club progressed rapidly and by 1957 membership had grown to about sixty members.

One of the main aims of the club was to foster friendliness and cooperation between those who were interested in hunting Bassets and those interested in showing. Mrs. Hodson was quoted as saying, "It would indeed be a tragedy if the present Club went the way of the old one. We want to breed Basset Hounds that retain the old characteristics but who are active and sound enough to hunt, in other words, hunting hounds that can win on the bench, and bench hounds

American Ch. Lyn Mar Acres End Man of Maycombe. Sired by Italian and American Ch. Lyn Mar Acres M'Lord Batuff ex Lyn Mar Acres BurLeeQ. Bred, first owned and shown by Margaret S. Walton; exported to Mildred Seiffert.

that can hunt in the field. I think the future of Bassets is bright, there is definitely an effort being made to breed sound, active, Bassets of the correct type and there is a friendly spirit between breeders, exhibitors and Basset owners generally.''

Most certainly Miss Keevil's Grims Hounds and Mrs. Hodson's Rossingham Bassets have played a great part in improving the breed worldwide.

Before World War II there can have been few, if any Bassets which were more than two generations away from pack hounds. Suddenly the breed flew into popularity and in 1965 Miss Keevil wrote, ''Now that the Basset Hound is experiencing a fashionable spell and one can even buy one in the larger London stores with the week's groceries and probably with far less consideration, it is inevitable that there are numbers of nervy (different from nervous) unhealthy and destructive Bassets dragging out their existence in homes only suitable for a small dog.'' She then goes on to write,

"If the instincts from pack ancestry persist, so too, do many less awkward ones and the day these characteristics are bred out, then there will be no more Basset Hounds, only another variety of dog to show and sell to the public, price graded, no doubt, according to length of ear, the Basset. Remember, every bitch puppy sold is a probable brood bitch, whether the seller has that wish for its future or not. The placing of such a bitch puppy should be considered a serious responsibility.''

Today the Basset Hound Club is an extremely strong and workable club with Mrs. Mildred Seiffert as chairman and Mr. Michael Errey as vice-chairman, both show and field are well taken care of. Their regional clubs are known as ''branches'' of which there are eight, with the Albany Basset pack making it nine. Each branch sends its own newsletter and lists its activities. Each branch has a representative on the committee of the Basset Hound Club.

Maycombe Diorama By Moonsmead Winthrop (grandson of Ch. L.M.A. End Man) ex Maycombe Dixie (daughter of Ch. L.M.A. End Man) Bred, owned and shown by Mildred Seiffert (Maycombe Kennels) and Joan Izard (Moonsmead Kennels).

The Club also has a rescue service under the guidance of Mr. Nick Frost who is well known for both Basset Hounds and Petit Basset Griffon Vendeens. This is a very worthwhile endeavor.

A number of books have been written by English breeders in the last three decades; all make wonderful reading and give great advice. George Johnston (Sykemoor), Joan Wells-Meacham (Fredwell), Jeanne Rowett-Johns (Wingjays) and Douglas H. Appleton (Appeline) all offer their experiences and helpful hints. Some of these books are now out of print and have become collectors' items.

A great many Bassets have come to our shores but fewer have gone to England due in part to the six-months quarantine. Those sent over seem to have made quite a mark on the British Basset— how permanent this will be remains to be seen. A total outcross should always be well thought out as one never jumps from the frying pan into the fire.

AUSTRALIA

Bassets have been in Australia since before 1900, but never caught hold and thus the breed had died out.

In 1950, Dr. and Mrs. Harry Spira and Mr. and Mrs. John McInulty decided to import some Bassets from England, as they seemed to be a breed that would be interesting. Their first was a bitch from Peggy Kevil named Grims Caroline, very much in whelp. Dr. Spira gives a most interesting account of early temperament!

Also entering the new continent were Mr. and Mrs. Hurling, from England, whose Majesty Kennel bred some fine, early hounds; Mrs. Hurling is still in the breed and continues her love for them in the show ring. Janet Beckman, Margaret Webber, Mr. and Mrs. Poulton and Mr. and Mrs. Keith McGinn all have contributed to the popularity of the breed today.

The quality has been kept very high by dedicated breeders, and although there is a nine-month quarantine for a dog coming from America, a few have braved this. Mrs. Webber imported Am. Ch. Vahhala's Retsof Slugger from Mr. and Mrs. Wagner, and Mr.

Aus. Ch. Ammidan Far Lancelot (Aus. Ch. Verwood Ruggles—U.K. ex Aus. Ch. Ammidan Paw Melody) was shown at the Basset Hound Show of Queensland in the Minor Puppy Dog Class and won the Challenge Certificate and Best of Breed. A year later at the same Specialty Lancelot was awarded Best of Breed again. He is a multi-Group and Best in Show winner, owned and shown by Keith McGinn of Australia.

Mr. and Mrs. Keith McGinn's kennels at Ammidan, Queensland, Australia.

156

and Mrs. McGinn had Lyn Mar Acres The Gambler sent out. Many hounds had come from England so that the crossing of these various lines have proven to be highly satisfactory. So much so that Best in Show 1992, at the Brisbane Royal with nearly 5,000 dogs entered, went to a son of The Gambler, bred and owned by the McGinns. More will undoubtedly be heard from this Basset, Ch. Ammidan Casino Royale.

NEW ZEALAND

Being in such close proximity to Australia, it stands to reason that much of the breeding is similar. This country has some very fine breeders on both the North and South Islands as well as active regional breed clubs and a strong parent club. Specialties are well attended and quality high.

THE CONTINENT

France and Belgium were the original stronghold countries of the Basset and so we would expect the breed to have slowly filtered into other European countries. We find enthusiastic breeders in Switzerland, and strong breed clubs in Germany, Italy and Holland. Many of the Bassets taken into these countries were of English origin, probably because of the easy access to various breeders in that country. Some, however, did import from America with good results. Holland has a number of hounds from Mr. and Mrs. Henry Jerman's Tally-Ho Kennel. Grace Servais of Switzerland has taken back interesting breeding stock on her visits to the Basset Hound Club of America National Specialties.

Italy had very strong supporters in Rita Rossi and Dr. Giuseppe Benelli. Both maintained strong breeding programs and drew from Canadian, American and English bloodlines. Mildred Seiffert (England) and your author were privileged to share the judging of Bassets at the World Show 1980, in Verona, Italy. Two different rings, same judging time, Mrs. Seiffert doing bitches, while the

Grim's Ulema De Barly—Basset Artesien Normand
Sire: Sans-Souci de Bourceville
Dam: Querelle de Barly
Imported from France into England by Peggy Keevil (Grims)
(Thomas Fall photo)

dogs and intersex were judged by Margaret S. Walton. The results were brother and sister of Fredwell breeding from the same kennel.

SCANDINAVIA

Finland, Norway and Sweden have long been a three-country alliance in Bassets. Exhibitors from Norway and Sweden go freely back and forth across the border for shows or breeding, making it slightly easier to maintain a balance of good dogs from a wider gene pool. Imports have moved freely into these two countries with only a four-month quarantine. Mrs. R. M. Hartvig was an early breeder in Sweden, importing from both America and England. Dr. Andrews, now living in Sweden, may very well help the breed along with her Langpool prefix.

Norwegian Ch. Lyn Mar Acres Brass Top by Ch. Lyn Mar Acres Sir Michelob ex Ch. Lyn Mar Acres Lovage. Owned by Elizabeth Knapp, Baseknap Kennels, Norway.

In Norway, Elizabeth Knapp (Baseknap) had shown Frida to her championship. She was a granddaughter of two English imports Swed.-Nor.-Danish Ch. Hardacre Domino and Swed.-Nor.-Finnish Ch. Chantinghall Lancer. Ms. Knapp then purchased Lyn Mar Acres Brass Top, who became a Norwegian champion. She then obtained the English bitch Verwood Water Bride, sired by Am. Ch. Lyn Mar Acres End Man ex Wellshim Carmen, a litter sister to Eng. Ch. Wellshim Cruiser, which had been put up for dog Challenge Certificates from the puppy class at Windsor. Doing intense linebreeding Ms. Knapp's dogs produced very well, although business matters have kept her from the show ring. Baseknap Outlaw has been sent to the States and is siring well from the Lyn Mar Acres line.

Finland has an active club headed by Marita Massingberd. Interested in both show and field trials, Marita balances both in her businesslike way and makes a great success of it all. Having had Bassets for many years, she has added a new challenge, Basset Artesien Normand. She is still active with Bassets and the Club and hopes to remain so.

Ch. Bugle Bay's Souffle, UD, is credited with 8 High in Trial wins, 39 Field points, 40 OT Championship points. Proudly owned by James A. and Margery Cook, Bugle Bay Bassets.

12

Basset Hounds in Obedience and Agility

by Kay Green

THOSE WHO KNOW the Basset Hound may find it difficult to associate this breed with the word "obedient." By their very nature as hunting hounds, Bassets were bred to stick to a trail of scent without distraction. Being mostly concerned with their own pleasure, they tend to use their tenacity toward their own ends, rather than pleasing their owners or trainers. This does not usually include Obedience. There are some other breeds who have been selectively bred for their willingness to be obedient and to enjoy whatever makes their humans happy. So, when a person who enjoys the sport of Obedience makes a decision about the breed of dog to train, the Basset Hound does not usually come to mind. There have been some fine working Bassets who give other breeds a run for their money in class placements, but they are few and far between.

Most people who train Bassets *and* acquire Obedience titles, do so because they love the breed and happen to enjoy Obedience. Achieving Obedience titles on a hound can be a rewarding experience, even with no thought of high scores or class placements. There is room in the sport of Obedience for all who are interested, whether for fun or glory.

TRAINING METHODS

There are many training methods for Obedience. You can find seminars on how to best train your dog almost any month of the year if you are willing to travel. Unfortunately, most people who run these seminars have little or no experience in training hounds as a group or Bassets as a breed. Their methods are usually rather harsh for this breed and often cause Bassets to "dig in" their heels and resist this kind of forceful training.

The best rule of thumb for training this breed: If what you are doing is helping your hound to learn a particular exercise and the dog is enjoying it, then you have hit upon the right method. Listen to your dog, not to so-called experts who have rarely, if ever, worked with a hound.

This will probably mean learning to be very *inventive* in your training methods and changing them from time to time, as the Basset gets bored. This is not as difficult as it first may seem. In fact, it can be the most fun and creative part of the sport. You will be the envy of your area as you drag around all different kinds of training equipment and show others that this breed can work in Obedience, do it well and have a good time doing it! Watching other trainers who are successful training sensitive, difficult-to-train dogs is one very good way to get some ideas to try. Many physically handicapped Obedience trainers have had to invent their own methods; you can learn a lot from them. There are a lot of people training and showing Bassets in Obedience—if you get stuck give one or all of them a call. Most people are happy to help.

If your Basset starts to slow down and show resistance to working, this usually means that the dog either has become bored or has something else better to do, or you may have been given some bad training advice. Whatever the reason, a good cure is to be training two dogs at the same time. Because of the Bassets' competitive nature, they perk right up when they see you having a good time working another dog. It usually works best if the first one you train one week becomes the last one the next week. Keep them guessing!

Obedience has been around for a long time and Bassets have been right there with other breeds. Over the years many people have found methods that work for them and have enjoyed many hours of training and showing. When training Bassets, you really have to love the sport of Obedience because you only spend a few minutes in the ring at shows, compared to the hundreds of hours spent training for those few minutes.

AKC OBEDIENCE TITLES

For those of you who have never been exposed to the sport of Obedience, a summary of what you can expect follows. For more information on the specific requirements of each title, it is a good idea to obtain a copy of the American Kennel Club (AKC) Obedience Regulations.

Sketches of some of the equipment used in Obedience are shown in these regulations, as well as a detailed description of each exercise. To achieve *each* of the three regular Obedience titles offered by the AKC, three separate qualifying performances must be achieved under three separate judges and in at least three Trials.

Under the auspices of the AKC, three regular Obedience titles and an Obedience Trial Championship (OTCH) may be earned.

Companion Dog

The first level of training for a title is called Novice and consists of **Heeling on- and off-lead** (your dog's shoulders should be in line with your left leg), **Figure-8, Stand for Examination, Recall** (having your dog come to you on command) and the group **Sit-Stay** and **Down** exercises. The Figure-8 exercise includes a pattern in which dog and handler heel around two other people. The title earned at the Novice level is the Companion Dog (CD) degree.

Ch. Bugle Bay's Bouillon, CDX, TD; sired by Ch. Harper's Rhett Butler ex
Ch. Bugle Bay's Ado Annie, CD. Bred and owned by Jim and Marge Cook.

Companion Dog Excellent

The next title, Companion Dog Excellent (CDX), involves a
higher level of training in order to prepare you both for the exercises.
This second level of Obedience is referred to as the Open level. For
this title all of the exercises are done off-lead. The lead is left at the
ring entrance with the steward until after you have completed all of
the required exercises.

These exercises include the **Heel Off-Lead, Figure-8, the
Drop-on-Recall** (Down command given during the Recall exercise)
and the **Retrieve** of a dumbbell **on the Flat** *and* **Over the High**

Ch. Pinebrooks Apollo, CDX, TDX. This dog and Ch. Strathalbyn Last Call are the only two dogs holding all of these AKC titles.

Jump. During this last exercise, the dog must jump a short High Jump going out for the dumbbell and also coming back to the handler. The height of this jump is equal to the Basset's height at the withers or shoulders (some breeds jump higher).

The last exercise before the group Stay exercises is the Broad Jump, in which you must be standing at the side of the Broad Jump boards and have your dog jump over the middle of them, turn and sit in front of you. For our breed, two or three flat boards are used, (depending on the height of the dog at the withers) supported at an angle and placed one in front of the other. This exercise sounds hard to train for, and can be if you are not creative. However, the use of training aids such as guides and barriers for the dog can make this exercise one of your best. The group **Stays** are done with handlers out of sight of the dogs, and last longer than the Novice group exercises.

Utility Dog

The highest regular Obedience title your dog can achieve is the Utility Dog (UD) title. The exercises at this level can be very challenging for both trainer and dog. They can also take a fairly long time to adequately prepare a Basset for a show. It is the most fun and exciting title, but it requires an extraordinary Basset Hound and persistent trainer.

These exercises are all off-lead and include the **Signal Exercise**. This means during off-lead Heeling, the judge tells you to stand your dog and leave. You then walk about 10 feet, turn, face your dog and wait until the judge signals you to signal the dog to **Drop** (Down), **Sit** and **Recall**. At that time the judge will have you Finish your dog. This is the final movement of the dog back into the Heel position. All the different parts of this exercise (including the Heeling) are done with *hand signals only*—no voice commands are permitted.

The next Utility exercise is the Retrieve of a leather *and* a metal article or dumbbell by **Scent Discrimination**. Several articles are placed on the floor by the ring steward and will therefore have the steward's scent on them. Your dog is to look for, find and return

Ch. Bugle Bay's Souffle, UD by Ch. Lane's Arlo of Castlereagh ex Ch. Le Clair's Merry Madelyn, UD. Bred and owned by Jim and Marge Cook.

only the ones with your scent on them. The dog will be sent twice: once to find the correct leather article and once for the metal. A similar exercise is the **Directed Retrieve**, where the dog is directed by hand signal to one of three gloves set out along the back of the ring, and must retrieve only the one signaled.

The moving **Stand for Examination** and **Return to Heel** are next. The first part of this exercise merely consists of heeling with your dog for a short distance and having the dog stand while you continue to walk away. You walk about 10 more feet, turn and face your dog. At this time the judge thoroughly examines your dog, then tells you to give the command to Finish. From the standing position, the dog is supposed to go directly to the Heel position and *not* sit in front of you like the other exercises that call the dog to come to you.

The **Directed Jumping** is next. On one side of the ring is a

Lena Wray with her bevy of Basset title-holders.

High Jump, and on the other side is a Bar Jump. You are to have your dog sitting by you in the Heel position at one end of the ring approximately in the middle, facing the area between the two jumps. On command from the judge you send your dog away from you, although the two jumps to the other side of the ring. Your dog is supposed to keep going until you give the command to Sit. At this time the dog should turn around at the far end of the ring and sit, facing the handler. The judge will indicate the jump toward which you are to send your dog. You can give a hand *and* voice signal to indicate which one to take. The dog is supposed to jump the *indicated jump* and return to you. The next part of the exercise is to do it all over again, but this time the dog will be instructed to take the opposite jump.

TITLES COMPLETED

For each of the three levels of Obedience described, the AKC issues specific titles, CD, CDX or UD. If you complete all of the above mentioned exercises three times for each title, at three different shows and under three different judges, then the American Kennel Club (AKC) will issue a certificate with your dog's name for each title earned.

OBEDIENCE TRIAL CHAMPION

The Obedience Trial Champion (OTCH) title is a very special one, for which only dogs who have already earned the Utility Dog (UD) title can compete. The dog must earn 100 points from the Open B and Utility B classes (if the Utility class is divided between A and B), with a First Place in each class along with an additional First Place in either class. The three First Places must be under three different judges at all-breed dog shows. For points to be earned, there must be at least three dogs competing in Utility and six dogs in Open B. This title is only for those special dogs that love competing in these classes over and over again and have the physical stamina and temperament to do a lot of traveling and frequent showing. The Basset is one breed that can find the repetition boring and the constant traveling and pressure to perform extremely stressful.

There have been a few Bassets who have earned OTCH points, but because of the extreme stress or other such factors, almost all have had to retire. To date there has been only one Obedience Trial Champion in this breed—OTCH Buzz Taylor's Goober. This was a very special dog indeed. To be an Obedience Trial Champion (OTCH) is considered by many people to have considerably more meaning than a breed championship because of the extremely difficult requirements to achieve it. This is a much-coveted title, as evidenced by the fact that only one Basset has achieved it.

Obedience with the Basset Hound can be both rewarding and frustrating, depending upon the dog, training schedule and interests of both dog and trainer. If you haven't tried Obedience you might be missing something that you and your Basset Hound would both enjoy. This is especially true for retired breed champions who miss

Champion Juley von Skauton, the first Basset Hound Agility titleholder, is proudly shown by Douglas C. Taylor, who co-owns her with Garry E. Towne.

the excitemednt of going places and being part of the dog show community.

AGILITY

One of the new and exciting aspects of dog sports is the Agility classes. It's fun watching dogs of all breeds climb up and over the A frame, use the teeter-totter, crawl through the tunnel and weave in and out of a waving line of brightly painted dowels—which are some of the things our intelligent four-footed companions are asked to do, and they truly enjoy it all.

To find a Basset Hound who is willing (and able) to do all these things is a rarity, but the breed can proudly say it now has its first Agility titled dog under the rules of the National Club for Dog Agility.

Ch. Juley von Skauton, Agility I, is proudly co-owned by Douglas C. Taylor, Switchstand Bassets, and Garry E. Towne, Von Skauton Kennel, and was shown by Doug Taylor, who writes: "Very much a Basset, Juley finished under *her* terms, not mine! She is not Obedience trained—only trained to come when off-lead. It has been a lot of fun, and she adores the cheering of the crowd when she climbs (struggles with gritted teeth) up over the A frame."

It is hoped that more Basset owners will join in the Agility fun and that their Bassets enjoy it as much as Juley does.

Kay and Craig Green obtained their first Basset Hound in 1972. Since then, they have both been actively involved in Conformation and Tracking, with Kay involved in Obedience as well. Between them, they have acquired ten breed championships, sixteen Tracking Dog (TD) titles and four Tracking Dog Excellent (TDX) titles. Both Kay and Craig have been past recipients of the Gaines Good Sportsmanship award by the Mountain States Dog Training Club.

Kay Green has trained ten Basset Hounds, a Wirehaired Dachshund and a Fox Terrier to their Companion Dog (CD) titles. In addition, she has acquired five Companion Dog Excellent (CDX) titles and one Utility Dog (UD) title on her Basset Hounds. Several of her hounds have been nationally ranked for their Obedience work. In 1980, one of Kay's Basset Hounds was awarded the Dog World Award of Canine Distinction for obtaining three consecutive scores of 195 or higher, out of a maximum score of 200 points. In 1982, she completed the last title on the only Basset Hound ever to have acquired six AKC titles: Ch. Winnwars Brandywine, UDTX.

Ch. Winnwars Brandywine, UDTX, proudly displaying his awards for the sixth and last AKC title, Tracking Dog Excellent (TDX). Owned by Kathryn Green.

13

Tracking with the Basset Hound

by Craig Green

THE AMERICAN KENNEL CLUB (AKC) sport of Tracking is one of the most satisfying activities in which a Basset Hound owner can participate. The close bond that develops between hound and handler through the communication of a long leash in the field is unparalleled. It must be experienced to be fully appreciated!

WHAT IS TRACKING?

AKC tracking is a *noncompetitive sport* that requires a dog to follow an unmarked course of human scent through a field, finding one or more articles dropped by the tracklayers. The handler follows the dog at a distance between 20 and 40 feet, with a long leash providing constant communication.

At a licensed Tracking Test, each dog/handler team draws by lot a different track, which was plotted and staked by two judges on

Jagersven Grace Berry Brown, TD. Owned and handled by Lena Wray, shown with judges Patricia and Richard Norris.

the previous day. On the day of the test, the designated tracklayer walks the track, leaving one or more personal articles for the dog to find. All markers are removed except for the starting flag(s), so that neither dog nor handler knows where the track leads after the start. A Tracking trial is a single pass/fail test in which the dog may earn either the Tracking Dog (TD) or Tracking Dog Excellent (TDX) title. Basset Hounds are well suited for Tracking because of their breeding and selection as hunting hounds.

TD trials consist of tracks between 440 and 500 yards in length, usually with three to five turns. At least thirty minutes after the tracklayer walks the track, the dog/handler team is shown the starting flag by the judges. A single article, found at the end of the track by the dog, completes a passing performance.

TDX trials consist of tracks between 800 and 1000 yards in length, usually with five to seven turns. Tracks are aged a minimum of three hours, with at least two obstacles such as road, creek or fence crossings. A TDX track has four articles, all of which must be found. About one and a half hours after the track is laid (walked), two cross-tracklayers walk across the track perpendicular to it, at two different places on the track. The dog must get beyond these purposely difficult encounters, and successfully complete the *correct* track. Like the Utility Dog title in Obedience, the Tracking Dog Excellent title is only for the exceptional dog. This is shown by the relatively few dogs that have acquired it—fewer than one out of five entered.

THE PEOPLE

Tracking people are generally the most friendly and supportive of all those who participate in dog sports. Perhaps this is because of the noncompetitive nature of the Tracking event. There are no scores, ratings or placements in AKC Tracking. The pass/fail system means that one dog/handler team's success does not diminish the accomplishments of others.

Several Basset Hound trainers have been continuously involved with Tracking for a number of years, like Sue Boyd (Missouri),

Marge Cook (Texas), Joan Deibler (Pennsylvania), Sally Elkins (Texas), Kay and Craig Green (Colorado), Ben Harris (California), Bill Lindsay (Illinois), John and Elaine McDowell (Illinois), Doc and Ruth Paule (North Carolina), Florence Voigt (Arizona) and Lena Wray (Florida). Many others too numerous to mention have also found the combination of Bassets and Tracking to be irresistible. At this writing, five Basset trackers are licensed AKC Tracking judges: Lena Wray (TDX), Sally Elkins (TDX), Sue Boyd (TDX), Craig Green (TDX) and Florence Voigt (TD).

TDX BASSET HOUNDS

The extreme commitment it takes to acquire a TDX title makes it one of the most difficult (but rewarding) to achieve. As of the summer of 1992, only eighteen Basset Hounds had acquired the elusive TDX title:

TDX Basset Hounds as of July 1992:

1. Brownridge Bootlegger, CD, TDX, Can. TDX, Bda. TD
   Owned by Susan A. and Thomas Boyd
2. Governor M. McDuffy, CDX, TDX
   Owned by Sally B. Davis
3. Bee Lee's Tracking Schooze, CD, TDX
   Owned by Sally J. Elkins
4. Ch. Winnwars Brandywine, UDTX
   Owned by Kathryn J. Green
5. Dig 'Em Widetrack, CD, TDX
   Owned by Joyce A. Capoccia
6. Arrowstone Earth Angel Clara, TDX
   Owned by Linda and Herbert E. Brown
7. Gerianne's Esther Marie, UDTX
   Owned by Gerianne F. and George W. Darnell
8. Branscombe's Aldonza, TDX
   Owned by William Lindsay
9. Capriole Muddy Brown Sneaker, TDX
   Owned by Kathleen Scott and Barbara Hall

Bev-Lee's Tracking Schooze, CD, TDX. This is the first Basset bitch to earn a TDX. Owned by Sally Elkins, bred by Lena Wray.

10. Ch. Chez Bonheur Ante-Bellum, CD, TDX
    Owned by Susan A. Boyd
11. Roadway's Rambling Rogue, CDX, TDX
    Owned by Dietrich and Florence Voigt
12. Gendarme B. J. Gum Schooze, TDX
    Owned by Sally J. Elkins

Ch. Winnwars Brandywine, UDTX. The Breed's *first* Ch. UDT and UDTX. His last title was earned in 1982 and he is still the only holder of all six titles after 10 years. Owned by Craig and Kay Green.

13. Ch. Strathalbyn Last Call, CDX, TDX
    Owned by Kay Green
14. Ch. Pinebrook's Apollo, CDX, TDX
    Owned by Kay and Craig Green

Ch. Strathalbyn Last Call, CDX, TDX, a grandson of Ch. Strathalbyn Shoot-To-Kill, CD, TD, after passing his TDX test in Albuquerque. Owned by Kay Green. This dog and Ch. Apollo are the only holders of all of these titles.

15. Condas Golden Brutus, CD, TDX
   Owned by Connie Sue Canfield and David P. Titter
16. Brierwoods Musical Schooze, TDX
   Owned by Sally J. Elkins

17. Stillhouse Abigail, TDX
    Owned by James A. and Margery B. Cook
18. Tuff Tizzy Samantha, CDX, TDX
    Owned by Margaret E. Haselden

TRAINING THE BASSET HOUND TO TRACK

A comprehensive training method would require a complete book to fully describe, but a few ideas are presented here that may help prospective Basset Hound trackers get started.

The Basset Hound Club of America (BHCA) publishes a booklet (authored by Ruth Paule) that contains an excellent introduction to the sport and specific training methods for Bassets. Its title is *Tracking with a Basset Hound: A Guide for All Basseteers.* Also, Sue Boyd has co-authored a book on TDX training with her friend and fellow judge Sandy Ganz, entitled *Tracking Dog Excellent: A Handbook* (St. Louis: Show-Me Publications). Both are excellent sources of training information.

Ch. Pinebrooks Apollo, CDX, TDX, showing how it is done!

Ch. Strathalbyn Legacy, TD earned a Tracking title under judges Helen Hittesdorf and Sue Effinger. Owned by Kay and Craig Green.

The Basset Hound was originally bred to hunt small game, especially the European hare and cottontail. With short legs to allow hunters to follow on foot, long ears to aid in scenting and loose skin that will easily disengage from thorns, the proper Basset Hound displays the natural ability and elegance of an athletic hunter. Equipped with one of the finest scenting noses ever developed by selective breeding, the Basset Hound is a natural candidate for Tracking. While the hound is typically good at scenting and independent problem solving, a sometimes stubborn temperament often leads to training problems in Tracking. Training a Basset to track is almost always based on finding and providing the proper motivation.

Training a Basset Hound involves a commitment of time, energy and respect for a particular hound's temperament and ability. The most important lesson a new trainer can learn is not to inhibit the hound's natural ability and desire to put nose to ground and follow scent.

The specific motivational goal is to teach the hound that there

Jagersven Bluejay, TD resting after his 'find.' Owned by Lena Wray.

is something desirable to find at the end of the track. Beginning with short tracks of a few steps, the new Tracking hound is gradually taught to use his/her nose to follow a human scent over a distance of several hundred yards in order to find the article at the end (usually a leather glove). Food or a favorite toy on the article may be used to motivate the dog in training, although such aids are not permitted at a Tracking Trial.

The best way to learn to track is to work with an experienced trainer—preferably someone who has worked with Basset Hounds before. As with Obedience, training methods that work for other breeds don't always produce good results for hounds. Consideration for the individual dog is the key to motivating intelligent but stubborn hounds. Basset Hound trainers sometimes learn more from their dogs than the dogs learn from trainers!

Ch. Strathalbyn Shoot-To-Kill, CD, TD, shown tracking. Owned by Kay and Craig Green. Michael is the only top winning Basset Hound to ever hold both Obedience and Tracking titles.

Tracking the Basset Hound can be an invigorating experience. However, the hound's temperament requires a patient, gentle approach to training, based almost entirely on motivation. A careful consideration for the abilities and desires of the individual hound will likely bring the trainer many hours of satisfying accomplishment in the field.

As a sport in the truest sense of the word, Tracking with a Basset Hound combines the hound's love for field work with a unique working bond between dog and handler. The joy and satisfaction of Basset Tracking can be matched only by the sound of a hunting pack at full cry!

Craig Green has been a Tracking judge since 1985, having judged over forty Tracking Tests and Tracking Dog Excellent (TDX) trials. He has taught several Tracking seminars, including tracklaying, map drawing, lead handling and problem solving. He will begin writing the Tracking column for Talley-Ho, *the Basset Hound Club of America magazine, in 1993.*

Westminster—1955   Judge: Alva Rosenberg
Ch. Greenore's Joker—handler, Johnny Davis
Second Best in Show winner in U.S.A.
Lyn Mar Acres Top Brass—Breeder, owner, handler Margaret S. Walton
Best of Breed over 7 specials at 9 months of age
Both dogs were sons of Ch. Lyn Mar's Clown

14

"If Wishes Were Horses . . ." Reflections on the Past

THERE ARE ALWAYS those you wish you *had* met and those you are glad you *did*. How I would love to have had a long conversation with Sir Everett Millais; reading his book on *The Theory and Practice of Rational Breeding* (1889) is as near as anyone will come. What a worthwhile addition to your research library. How he was able to write as he did without resentment or even a lawsuit baffles one.

Time spent with the Heseltines, especially Captain Godfrey, would have made my day. How they bred such great type with ability in the field—and could I possibly purchase that lead hound Walhampton Galliard and the bitch running in the middle of the pack—Walhampton Dauntless, a Ch. Bourbon granddaughter? What quality!! I am so thankful for the hounds descended from them.

Ch. Lyn Mar Acres Top Brass winning Best of Breed at the Basset Hound Club of America National Specialty from the Veteran class. Topper was 7½ years of age. Carol Stewart was the judge.

And that great lady Peggy Keevil who saved the breed from oblivion in England during World War II, keeping the nucleus of her pack going by every means possible. My first visit to England many years ago gave me the opportunity to not only meet but spend time with her, walk the hounds, hold my beloved Denny (Lyn Mar Acres Dauntless) on my lap and help whelp a new litter. A more gracious, dedicated lady I have never met and I respect her as no other.

Irene and Harold Fogleson of Greenly Hall fame were not only kind but great teachers and always a font of information and suggestions.

Mr. and Mrs. Gerald Livingston will always be remembered for opening their kennel after fifteen years so that two neophytes, willing to learn and abide by the rules, could obtain a long lost bloodline. We learned more in two afternoons with Mr. Livingston than we did from all the books we had read.

Ch. Abbot Run Valley Brassy, by Ch. Lyn Mar Acres Top Brass ex Ch. Ro-Fre la Reine de la Balle, bred by Roger C. Fredette and co-owned with Walter F. Brandt.

Mr. and Mrs. Andrew Porter let us breed to their new import, and when the bitch produced six male puppies and I screamed ''Help!'' Betty laughed and said to keep what I wanted and sell the balance. No written agreement, just a handshake and trust.

Fred Bayless, one of the early breeders, would walk up and down the kennel row demanding to know why we had kept this one or that one, then nodded when we gave the right answer.

Consuelo Ford, of Bijou of Banbury pack, parted with Basso of Banbury to a gentleman from Staten Island who insisted we should own this hound in his old age. He was a wonderful addition to our breeding program.

Roger C. Fredette approached me in 1959 and asked about breeding his Ch. Ro-Fre la Reine de la Balle to Ch. Lyn Mar Acres Top Brass. Roger not only owned Reine but was indeed the breeder of Ch. Abbot Run Valley Brassy. Since he lived with Walter and Margery Brandt at that time, Brassy became a joint venture, although

Roger showed him to his wins. We are proud and happy to consider him and his wife, Lucille, our very dear and close friends after all these years—and they still have a Basset as a house dog!

To all friends and acquaintences worldwide, may you keep the quality of the breed sound and high, remember the purpose for which it was bred and love and enjoy the Basset Hound as much as we have, for *your* fifty years.

Glossary

TERMINOLOGY

A common error made by both the novice and some of our more seasoned breeders is terminology. How often have you heard, "She is *out of* Ch. Blank-Blank and her dam is Ch. So-So"? Just try getting a male to give birth to a litter. Anatomically it is impossible for that puppy to be "out of" a male—it is *by* the sire and *out of* the dam. So much for that lesson.

I have always maintained that you never enjoy any litter as much as your first! All the puppies are champions in your eyes, none of them have faults and all are big, bouncy, outgoing kids to be proud of—and they are "your breeding"—*Wrong*! It is a common fallacy that because you bred the litter they are *your* breeding, but one has only to look at the pedigree to realize someone else has done your homework and you have come along for the ride. Many years ago I stood watching Bassets being judged and a very pretty bitch went up shown by a lady who was obviously new to the breed and the show ring. After she savored that first thrill of victory I congratulated her, asking what the breeding was. She responded with, "It's all my breeding." Later, at home, I checked the catalog only to find that the sire was another kennel's bloodline and the dam was generations of ours!

Some years ago a young couple was sent a six-week-old Basset by the sister of the young man. Knowing nothing about the breed, or for that matter about raising a puppy, she called a friend of ours, the Master of Foxhounds for a well-known pack, who forwarded them to me. When the couple arrived, I took one look at a six-week-old Basset going on twelve weeks. I had never seen such an overdone baby in my life, but he seemed happy and healthy enough. I suggested a feeding and careful exercise program so they would not overdo and ruin the puppy. He came on very well and we all became good friends through "Plush." At a later time this couple had to make a business trip to the West Coast and asked if Plush could join our crew for a week while they were gone. Upon their return they reported they had run into the owner of the sire at a party, and she was very interested in the puppy's progress and where he had been left. When they replied that he was visiting Mrs. Walton for the week, the owner was most interested in what I thought of him. Bob stated that he was growing up well enough but Mrs. Walton said he was "low in the meadow." "Obviously an East Coast expression" was the retort. I thought about this for a few seconds before the dawn broke—"No, Bob, what I really said was he was down in the pastern!"

So much for terminology . . .

GLOSSARY

AKC: American Kennel Club.
ANGULATION: The angles formed by a meeting of the bones of the shoulder, upper arm, thigh, stifle and hock.

BAD MOUTH: Overshot, undershot, wry or misaligned teeth. (*See also* Mouth.)
BAY: The deep, prolonged voice of a hound, usually while trailing.
BITCH: A female dog.

BLANKET: The solid color of the coat on back and sides between the neck and tail.

BLOOM: The shine of the coat of a hound in top condition.

BREEDER: The registered owner of the dam (or the lessee) when the dam was *bred* to produce the litter.

BROKEN-EAR: The markings on the hound's ear or ears, usually two distinct colors, i.e., solid tan, brown or black with white splotch or heavy ticking.

BROOD BITCH: A female used for breeding.

BRUSH: The tail, heavy with hair, usually on the underside.

BULL NECK: A heavy, short neck, overly muscled.

CAT FOOT: Short, compact foot like that of a cat. Not to be appreciated in a Basset.

CHAMPION (Ch.): A prefix used with the name of a dog who has won 15 points under three different judges; at least two of these wins must be 3-point wins or better. Show win points range from one through five, depending on the number defeated.

CLODDY: Low, thick set, heavy, unable to gait easily.

COUPLE: Two hounds; also called a Brace.

COW-HOCKED: The hocks turn in toward each other.

CREST: The arch of the neck.

CRYPTORCHID: The adult whose testicles are retained and have not descended into the scrotum. Unilateral or monorchid is when one testicle has descended and one is retained or hidden.

DAM: The mother of the litter.

DEWCLAW: An extra toe on the inside of the leg. These are removed by some breeders.

DEWLAP: Loose, pendulous skin under the throat. Called for in the Basset Standard.

DOCK: To shorten the tail by cutting. *Not* allowed in a Basset.

DOG: The male of the species although used to designate both sexes.

DOWN IN PASTERN: Weak or faulty metacarpus, set at a pronounced angle from the vertical.

FIDDLE FRONT: Forelegs out at elbows, knees close, feet turn well out (east-west front).

FLEWS: Upper lips pendulous and rather heavy.

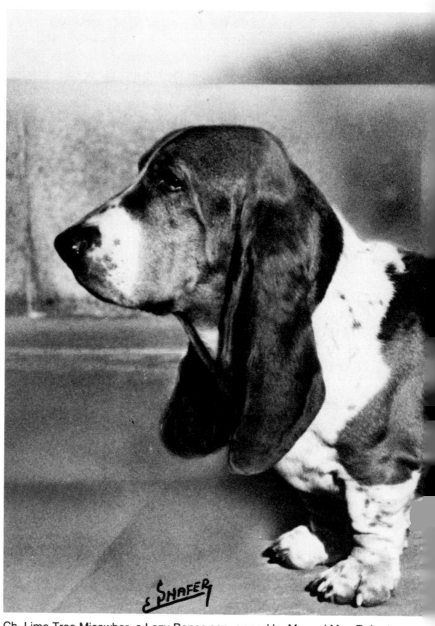

Ch. Lime Tree Micawber, a Lazy Bones son, owned by Mr. and Mrs. Robert V. Lindsay.

Shafer

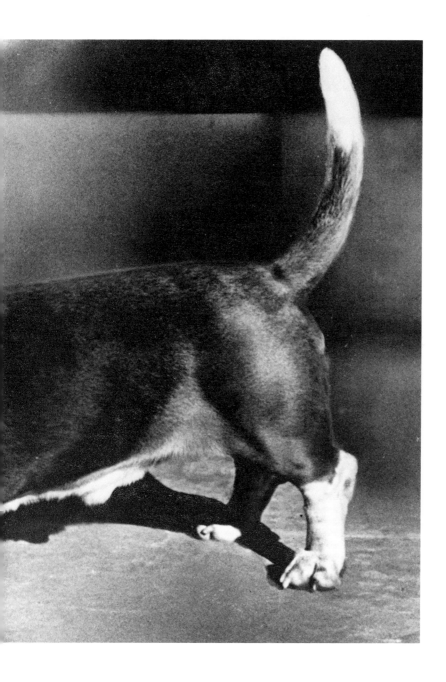

HARE FOOT: An elongated foot, e.g., like that of a hare or rabbit.

HAW: A third eyelid associated with the Basset and Bloodhound eye as well as some other breeds.

HOCKS: The bones of the hind leg forming the joint between the second thigh and the metatarsus.

HUMERUS (upper arm): The largest of the bones in the front assembly. When combined with the scapula, front angulation is formed.

INBREEDING: The mating of closely related dogs of the same breed, i.e., littermates, father-daughter, mother-son.

KNUCKLING (Knuckled over): Wrist joint (carpus) is defective, allowing it to double forward. Very noticeable in heavily boned Bassets.

LAYBACK (of shoulder): The angle of the shoulder blade as compared with the vertical. A "well laid back shoulder" should slant at 45 degrees to the ground forming a right angle with the humerus at the shoulder joint.

LEATHER: The flap of the ear. In pack hounds this refers to the entire ear.

LINEBREEDING: The mating of related dogs of the same breed. Usually with one or more common ancestors.

Intense Linebreeding: • Dog to granddam
                       • Bitch to grandsire
                       • Half brother and sister.

LOADED SHOULDERS: When the shoulder muscles are overdeveloped, the shoulder blades are pushed away from the body.

MONORCHID: *See* Cryptorchid.

MOUTH (Bite):

Scissors Bite: The outer side of the lower incisors touches the inner side of the upper incisors.

Level Bite: The front teeth edges of the upper and lower jaw meet perfectly.

Overshot (pig jaw): The front teeth of the upper jaw do not come in contact with the teeth of the lower jaw.

Undershot: The front teeth of the lower jaw protrude beyond the front teeth of the upper jaw.

Wry: The upper and lower jaws do not line up. The jaws can even be "twisted."

OCCIPITAL PROTUBERANCE: The bone (occiput) at the back point of the skull, which should be prominent, not rounded.

OCCIPUT: The back point of the skull.

OUT AT ELBOWS: Elbows turn outward from the body rather than lying in against the ribs.

OUTCROSSING: The breeding of totally unrelated individuals of the same breed.

PAPER FEET: Flat feet with very thin pads. Highly undesirable in a hound.

PASTERN: The bones between the waist (corpus) and the foot. A breed Standard will usually say whether these are to be sloping, upright or somewhere in-between, like the Basset Hound.

SCAPULA (the shoulder blade): The uppermost bone of the front assembly. A large, flat triangular bone helping to form the whithers.

SHORT COUPLED: Lacking the length of body and ribbing called for in the Basset Standard.

SPLAY FOOT: A flat foot with wide-open toes.

SPRADDLE REAR: With speed the hound moves wider in the rear in order to maintain balance, rather than moving in a normal manner. This can indicate stifle or hip problems.

STERN: The tail of the hound.

STERNUM: The breastbone. The Basset Standard calls for a ''prominent'' sternum, which is necessary for proper field work in heavy terrain.

STRAIGHT SHOULDER: The shoulder blades are straight up and down rather than being well laid back or at the 45 degree angle.

STUFFY: A hound is considered this when there is no length of neck and body, and it carries too much weight.

SUBSTANCE: The amount of bone.

TEAPOT TAIL: The tail goes straight up and curves over so that the tip touches the hound's back—or nearly so.

TICKING: Black or colored hairs sprinkled on the white of the hound.

TURN OF STIFLE: The angle taken by the joint of the hind leg between the thigh and the second thigh, as opposed to a straight stifle which has no bend and thus gives stilted movement.

UPPER ARM: The bone of the front quarters between the shoulder blade and forearm which should be approximately the same length as the shoulder blade to be in proper balance. A "short upper arm" restricts proper movement and makes for a choppy gait (see humerus).

WEEDY: A hound with insufficient bone and body structure.
WITHERS: The top of or between the shoulder blades (scapula); the highest point of the shoulder.

APPENDIX:

Kennel Names
Past and Present

ABBOT RUN VALLEY	Mr. and Mrs. Walter Brandt
	Mr. Roger C. Fredette
BAR-B	Barbara Dunning
BAYROC	Mr. and Mrs. Harry Porter
BEARTOOTH	Dr. and Mrs. Byron Wisner
BELBAY	Mr. Leslie Kelly
BEV-LEE	Mr. and Mrs. Lee Stockfelt
BLUE GRASS	Mr. and Mrs. William Spaulding
BLUE HILL	Mr. and Mrs. William Hurry
BRAUN'S	Mr. and Mrs. Joseph Braun
CAPE COD	Mr. and Mrs. Ray Wells
CASA FELICHE	Mr. and Mrs. Pete Balladone
CHERRY HILLS	Georgia White and Eric White
CORALWOOD	Mr. and Mrs. William Barton
CRAIGWOOD	Sandra Campbell
DARWIN	Ira Shoop
DELMAS	Patricia C. Kapplow
DIXIE'S	Mr. and Mrs. Tom T. Hall
DOUBLE-B	Mr. and Mrs. Clip Boutell

Ch. Oakway's Stormy of Howdot
Sire: Ch. Halcyon's Lochopt Letterman
Dam: Ch. Oakway's Sitting Pretty Almay
Breeders: J. P. Martinez and H. Hill
Owners/handler: Jaime P. and Frances Martinez.

ELEANDON	Eleanor Bliss
FOREST BAY	Mr. and Mrs. Joseph Kulper
GALWAY	Mr. and Mrs. Julian Dexter
GIN DIC	Virginia Lemeaux
GORHAM	Mabel Gorham
GREENLY HALL	Mr. and Mrs. Harold Fogleson
HARPER'S	Mr. and Mrs. Tom Harper
HARTSHEAD	Mr. and Mrs. Emil Seitz
HUBERTUS	Mr. and Mrs. Frank Hardy
HUNTING HORN	Mr. and Mrs. Charles Gillespie
JAGERSVEN	Mr. and Mrs. Finn Bergishagen
KAZOO	Mary Jo Shields
KILSYTH	Mr. and Mrs. Gerald Livingston
LONG VIEW ACRES	Chris Teeter
LOOK'S	Jean Look
LYN MAR ACRES	Mr. and Mrs. M. Lynwood Walton
MANDEVILLE	Helen Parkinson
MANOR HILL	Mr. and Mrs. Ronald Scholz
MARGEM HILLS	Mr. and Mrs. John Patterson
	Emily Kulchar

Ch. Lyn Mar Acres Ballyhoo and friend.

MILLVAN	Dr. and Mrs. Vincent Nardiello
MONA'S	Mona Ball
MUSICLAND	Jeanne Dudley Hills
NANCY EVANS	Nancy Evans
NORTHWOODS	Mr. and Mrs. Donald Martin
NOTRENOM	Mr. and Mrs. Richard Basset
ORANGE PARK	Mr. and Mrs. Wilton Meyer
RAN-SU	Susan A. Sutfin
RICHARDSON'S	David Richardson
ROCKIN-PAS	Paul Saucier
RUSSTAN	Mr. and Mrs. William Russell
SANTANA	Paul Nelson
SHOEFLY	Mr. and Mrs. Andy Shoemaker
SIEFENJAGENHEIM	Mr. and Mrs. John Siefen
SLIPPERY HILL	Mr. and Mrs. Leonard Skolnick
SMITH'S	Carl Smith
STANCO	Mr. and Mrs. Lewis Thompson
STONEYBLUFF	Mr. and Mrs. Frank Kovalic
SUPAI	Mr. and Mrs. Paul Mohr
TAL-E-HO	Mr. and Mrs. Henry Jerman
TALLEYRAND	Mr. and Mrs. Robert Ellenberger
TASON	Mr. and Mrs. Sonny Collee
THE RING'S	Mr. and Mrs. Robert Noerr
TOP-O-HIL	Mr. and Mrs. Curt Sheehy
UPLAND	Mr. and Mrs. Andrew Porter
VANCE'S	Rowland Vance
	Peggy Bowerman
WARWICK	Mr. and Mrs. Norman Bucher
WHITE MOUNTAIN	John Hackley
WINDMAKER	Mr. and Mrs. James White

200

Bibliography

Aldin, Cecil. *Dogs of Character*. England: Eyre & Spottis Woode Ltd. and Charles Scribner's Sons.

———. *An Artist's Models*. New York: Charles Scribner's Sons.

American Kennel Club. *The Complete Dog Book*. G. Howard Watt, Inc., Garden City Books; Howell Book House.

Barton, Frank Townend, MRCVS. *Sporting Dogs: Their Points and Management*. London: R. A. Everett & Co., Ltd.

Braun, Mercedes. *The New Complete Basset Hound*. New York: Howell Book House.

Bryden, H. A. *Hare, Hunting and Harriers*. London: Grant Richards.

———. *Horn and Hound*. Methuen & Co., Ltd.

Burges, Arnold. *The American Kennel and Sporting Field*. New York: Press of Jenkins & Thomas.

Carlson, D. G., DVM & Giffin, J., MD. *Dog Owner's Home Veterinary Handbook*. New York: Howell Book House.

Cobb, Bert. *Hunting Dogs*. New York: The Crafton Collection, Inc.

Collins, D. R., DVM. *The Collins Guide to Dog Nutrition*. New York: Howell Book House.

Cox, Herman. *Your Dachshund*. Hawthorne Books, Inc.

Daglish, E. Fitch. *The Basset Hound*. England: W. & G. Foyle, Ltd.

———. *Dachshunds*. England: Arco Publishing Co.

Ch. Tal-E-Ho's Top Banana (Ch. Tal-E-Ho's Prancer ex Tal-E-Ho's Dorinda), owned by Peter and Bryan Martin and bred by Henry Jerman and Mark Dembrow, was handled by his owners to numerous good wins in top national competition.   *Potter*

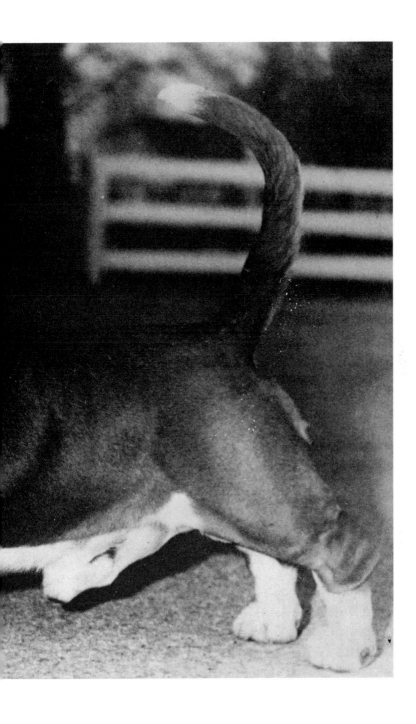

Davis, Henry P., ed. *The Modern Dog Encyclopedia*. New York: Stackpole and Heck, Inc.

Drury and others. *British Dogs*. London: L. Upcott Gill and New York: Charles Scribners.

Haynes, Williams. *Practical Dog Breeding*. Outing Publishing Co.

Heseltine, Capt. Godfrey. *The Basset Hound*.

———. "The Basset Hound." In *Dogs*, edited by Harding Cox. England: Fawcett, McGuire & Co.

Hubbard, Clifford. *Dogs in Britain*. England: Macmillan and Co. Ltd.

Hutchinson, Walter, ed. *Hutchinson's Dog Encyclopedia*. England: Hutchinson and Co., Ltd.

Johnston, George. *The Basset Hound*. London: Popular Dogs.

Lee, Rawdon R. *Modern Dogs*. London: Horace Cox

Livingston, Gerald M. "The Basset Hound." In *American Sporting Dogs*, edited by Eugene V. Connett. D. Van Nostrand Co., Ltd.

Marples, Theodore. *Show Dogs*.

Millais, Sir Everett. *The Theory and Practice of Rational Breeding*. England: "Fanciers Gazette" Ltd.

———. *The Basset Hound Club Rules and Stud Book*.

National Geographic Society. *The Book of Dogs*. Press of Judd & Detweiler, Inc.

———. *The National Geographic Book of Dogs*. The Lakeside Press R.R. Donnelley & Sons Company.

Rowett-Johns, Jeanne. *All About the Basset Hound*. London: Pelham Books, Ltd.

Smith, A. Croxton. *The Complete Book of Sporting Dogs*. London: TAPP & Toothill, Ltd.

———. *British Dogs at Work*. London: Adam and Charles Black.

———. *Sporting Dogs*. London: Hazell, Watson & Viney, Ltd.

Shaw, Vero. *The Classic Encyclopedia of the Dog*. New York: Crown Publishers Ltd. Originally published as *The Illustrated Book of the Dog*.

The Earl of Lonsdale, ed. *Deer, Hare and Otter Hunting*. London: Seely, Service & Co. Ltd. Basset chapter by Miss Ena Adams, Master for the Brancaster Basset Hounds.

———. *Hounds and Dogs*. London: Seeley, Service & Co. Ltd. Basset Hound chapter by Major Godfrey Heseltine.

Vesey-Fitzgerald, Brian, ed. *The Book of the Dog*. Bordon Publishing Co. Basset Hound chapter by Sheila Young.

Von Bylandt, H. G. *Hunderasen*. Germany: Verlag Buchhandlung Leopold
    Weiss Wein Und Leipzig.

Watson, James. *The Dog Book*. William Heinemann.

Woolner, Lionel R. *The Hunting of the Hare*. England: J. A. Allen & Co.
    Ltd.

The Kennel Club Stud Book 1883. England: Published for the Kennel Club.

American Kennel Register 1884, 1885, 1886, 1887. Forest & Stream
    Publishing Co.